# Life After Graduation
## *Your Guide to Success*
### Third Edition

By Terry J. Arndt & Kirrin R. Coleman

COLLEGE
**TRANSITION**
PUBLISHING
EST. 1999

# COPYRIGHT INFORMATION

# BOOK DISCLAIMER

College Transition Publishing has made its best effort in preparing this book to be accurate and complete. The content of the book is not guaranteed to produce any particular results. In addition, the advice given in the book may not suit every individual's circumstances.

Therefore, College Transition Publishing does not assume responsibility for advice given. As a result, each reader should consider their own circumstances and abilities and weigh them versus the advice given.

College Transition Publishing is not in the business of rendering financial, legal, or any other professional advice. If any questions regarding legal or financial advice should arise, the reader should seek professional assistance.

College Transition Publishing shall not be held liable for any damages arising from the book's content.

# About the Authors

**Terry J. Arndt**
Terry earned his Master of Business from the University of Florida. During his education, he found that sharing information with his classmates on how to achieve financial, career and academic success was extremely rewarding. As a result of his passion for helping others, Terry developed and launched College Transition Publishing during his MBA program. Since 1999, Terry has authored and published 15 publications, written numerous papers, and presented on hundreds of college campuses to tens of thousands of college students about achieving success during the college transition process. Terry is currently the President of College Transition Publishing (www.CollegeTransitionPublishing.com).

**Kirrin R. Coleman**
Kirrin has a Master of Arts in Education from Wake Forest University. She is a National Board Certified teacher who teaches English on Bainbridge Island, Washington. She is the coauthor and editor of *Life During College, Life During College-The Veteran's Guide to Success, Life During Community College, Life During College-The Online Learner's Guide to Success, Life After Graduation, Backpack to Briefcase*, and *Camo to Career*.

# ACKNOWLEDGMENTS

Financial and career advancement education, now more than ever, is an essential key to success for everyone – particularly college graduates. I have had the privilege to provide this information to hundreds of thousands of college graduates for more than 15 years.

The process of developing this publication was not accomplished alone. Kirrin Coleman, my co-author, continues to exceed expectations. Her ability to take detailed topics and break them down to the basics is phenomenal. In addition, Kirrin's ability to make reading a chapter on insurance entertaining is definitely unique. Of course, this publication would not have become reality without the hard work and superb design skills of Jeanette Alexander. Thank you both for your interest, dedication and support of this project.

Next, I would like to acknowledge and thank the thousands of colleges, students, and private organizations who have made College Transition Publishing a success. Your continued support, feedback and ideas over the years have been extraordinary.

Last, but definitely not least, I want to thank my parents (Mike and Rose), my wife (Joanna), family, friends, colleagues, and of course "bacon," for their continued support. The past couple years have been challenging to say the least – but together, you helped me come out of it a better, stronger and more confident man. Thank you!


*Terry J. Arndt*
President
College Transition Publishing

**✔ Here are ten things you can do *TODAY* to make sure your life after graduation is off to a good start:**

☐ Check out your credit report for free at **www.annualcreditreport.com**

☐ Identify two money leaks and fix them. *(see p. 17)*

☐ Cover yourself. Review your health and auto insurance policies to make sure you have appropriate insurance. *(see Chapter 4, p. 22 for more details.)*

☐ Know what you owe. How much do you owe? Who do you owe? What interest rates are you paying on your debts? What are the deadlines for paying those debts off?

☐ Make your privacy settings and passwords stronger.

☐ Google yourself.

☐ Set up or update your LinkedIn or Twitter account with your professional goals in mind.

☐ Set 5 short-term, 5 mid-range, and 5 long-range goals. *(see p. 45)*

☐ Become a member of a professional organization in your field.

☐ Check out your college's Career Services and Alumni Office websites to see what resources are available to you.

# TABLE OF CONTENTS

# INTRODUCTION

**Congratulations, graduate!** You are accomplished, educated, degreed, and ready to succeed in life. This transition period from student to professional can be both exhilarating and overwhelming. As your opportunities expand, so do the challenges. *Life After Graduation* will guide you through this process and help you achieve the success you desire.

You've mastered the art of student life: You can write a twenty-page paper in three hours, move all of your belongings in an afternoon, and stretch your budget like Laffy Taffy. You've memorized the library hours, as well as every other study area on campus, and learned where to get the best cheap eats in town. Of course, you also have knowledge of your subject area. You have skills. And chances are, you also have debt.

What you need now is a financial advisor, retirement planner, trusted insurance agent, career counselor, image consultant, marketing manager, and communications expert. And you need all the advice they have to offer as soon as possible. Well, look no further – we've done the legwork for you. We consulted experts in financial planning, insurance, and career development, then distilled everything they had to say about life after graduation into one little book. *Life After Graduation* covers all the relevant topics of this new phase of life – from what to expect of your first days on a new job to planning for retirement.

In these chapters you'll find answers to all your important questions – including some you might not have thought to ask. We'll address common questions, such as...

- What kind of insurance coverage do I need?
- How do I create a workable budget?
- How can I use credit cards wisely?
- Where can I find good—and inexpensive—financial and career advice?
- Why should I start investing in my retirement now?
- Should I consolidate my student loans?
- How can I make a great impression on my new boss and coworkers?
- What can I expect from my first few months on the job?
- How should I ask for a raise?
- How can I use my alumni connections to network?

Soon *you'll* be the expert on workplace culture and insurance riders and the best ways to trim your variable expenses. In the meantime, *Life After Graduation* will be your go-to resource, your quick and complete guide to the essential terms and concepts you need to understand as you transition from student to professional.

**Here's to your future!**

# CHECK YOUR CREDIT REPORT NOW!

**CHAPTER 1**

You are what you owe, what you buy, and how timely you pay your bills. And all that other stuff that makes you who you are—personality, gestures, intelligence, wit—means nothing to credit card companies, student loan agencies, landlords, loan officers, and even some employers. What matters most to them is simply the content and quality of your credit report. And if they like what they see, you advance to the next step, whether that's another student loan, a cool apartment, or a new job.

So, why is everyone so interested in your credit report? What does it reveal about you? Think of it as a credit report card that assesses your financial responsibility. First, it's a record of every time you apply for, or accept, a loan or other form of credit. Second, and more importantly, it keeps track of how you use your credit—how much you have available, how much you owe, and how you repay. The people who are considering hiring you, granting you a student loan, or giving you a new credit card simply want to know your financial track record.

## Credit Report & Credit Score —What Are They?

Your entire financial credit history is compiled by one of several credit bureaus and then organized into the following formats:

- **Credit Report:** A detailed history of your borrowing habits for the past seven to ten years, your credit report is a record of what you owe and to whom, what you've paid, and if you've made any late payments. It also reveals personal information, such as your social security number, current and former addresses and telephone numbers. Any time you order a report or authorize someone else to do so, the inquiry is recorded.

- **Credit Score:** A credit score is a shorthand way for a lender to tell if you're a good credit risk or a bad one. A high score means you're lower risk and have a better chance of obtaining the best interest rates. While each credit bureau has its own system, they all take into account the following five factors: your ability to make payments on time, the amount of credit you owe, the type of credit you owe, the length of your credit history (the longer, the better), and the number of requests for new credit.

### Who looks at my credit report?

Your landlord, employer, college, credit card company, bank, etc. all have an interest in reviewing your credit report.

**The three major credit agencies are:**

*Good To Know*

- **Equifax** (www.equifax.com)
- **Experian** (www.experian.com)
- **TransUnion** (www.transunion.com)

Do *you* know what your credit report contains? How much do you owe? Do you have any late payment history? Worse, is someone else using your identity to rack up debt? Before you do anything else, you need to check your credit report and credit score.

Many people don't see their own credit report until they are about to make a major purchase—or unless they're mysteriously turned down at one of those retail shops that practically throws credit cards at customers. Be proactive with your credit. Check it and address any problems immediately. Conventional wisdom says that it takes years to remove a blemish from a credit report, but seconds to put one on. While that may be an exaggeration, you don't want to be in the position to find out. In fact, it's wise to contact each of the three major credit reporting firms—they have different methods of reporting, so you want to know what they all say about you—and request a credit report every four months. This will enable you to monitor and prevent any illegal use of your credit.

## Review it, repair it, and get back on track

The first step to controlling your credit is to monitor it. The second step is to maintain and, if necessary, repair it. It's relatively easy to maintain and build your credit if you're starting with a strong foundation. Know what you owe, know who you owe, and pay your bills on time. If you move a lot, make sure every business you deal with has your change of address on file. Don't miss a payment because the vendor is sending bills to an old residence! Also, it's a

*TIP*

Order one free credit report every four months, rotating between the three major agencies. This is an inexpensive—free!—way to keep a close eye on your credit.

Ordering a credit report **DOES NOT** affect your credit score.

*Good To Know*

Applying for a credit card **DOES** affect your credit score.

good idea to set up a folder in your email account for e-bills, as they can easily get drowned in the in-box. Inadvertently missing a payment—even missing one because the vendor messed up—can cause as much headache as blatantly ignoring a due date.

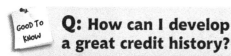

**Good To Know**

## Q: How can I develop a great credit history?

### A: Building credit is simple:
- ✔ **Get credit**
- ✔ **Use it**
- ✔ **Pay it off**

Don't make the mistake of not getting a credit card or never using the ones you have. Credit agencies want to see you have a history of good credit *use*.

Note: Identity theft is a real problem that can affect your credit for years. See Chapter 12 for more information about preventing and recognizing identity theft.

Repairing your credit is more challenging than maintaining it, but it's definitely a project you should start as soon as possible. Even if you have a poor track record, you can eventually recover your credit. Set up a system today for paying all current bills on time. If you have big outstanding balances that you can't pay off, contact the businesses to see if they'll negotiate a payment plan with you. Remember that vendors would rather have you pay them back directly than send your account to a collections agency, which would not only ding your credit but cost the vendor big money in lost revenue. (Collections agencies only return a small fraction of recovered payments to the original vendors.)

Paying attention to your credit now will pay off in the future, when you want to make a major purchase, such as buying a house. (The difference between an excellent credit score and a good credit score could be worth $100 or more a month on a 30-year fixed mortgage.) People with strong credit qualify for the best interest rates; you can take action now to make sure you're one of those people.

## Credit Repair

**To Do!**

Need help repairing your credit? Visit the Federal Trade Commission website (www.ftc.gov).

This government site takes the consumer step-by-step through the credit repair process. It includes a sample letter to send to creditors.

Other reliable resources include your local bank, financial advisor, even your college financial aid office—just ask!

### BEWARE!!!
**There is a credit repair mega-industry—legitimate as well as scamming—eager to prey on the unknowledgeable consumer. Read the FTC website before you begin your quest.**

# GET A GRIP ON YOUR FINANCES

## CHAPTER 2

Now's the time to get a grip on your finances. First, a quick quiz: Which of the following statements best sums up your financial situation at the end of each month?

a) "Hmm…should I put this extra $1,100 into savings or invest it in something with a greater return?"

b) "Mmm…Toasty-O's for dinner! Again."

c) "Um…do you think the landlord will take Visa?"

d) "Ahh…nothing beats selling plasma on a sunny afternoon!"

If you answered A, you can probably get away with skimming this chapter. Most Americans, however, are not socking away $1,100 a month. Many of us aren't putting away even $1 a month into savings of any kind. In fact, for a good part of the last decade, the personal savings rate was under 3%, while consumer debt soared. There are many people who do not have anything left over at the end of the month to save or invest. So, while you might not be selling plasma in that last week before payday, chances are you could use a budget.

Budget. Like its cousin *diet*, the word *budget* is often used and rarely implemented. Both are the subject of countless conversations, articles, self-help books, and advertisements. Yet, curiously, we don't live in a nation of rich, thin people. Or even healthy, debt-free people. Why the discrepancy? Well, everyone knows they *should* have a budget and *should* watch their diets, but many of us simply don't like *shoulds*. To many people, budgets and diets equal rules and restrictions: I *ought* to limit my spending, I *should* take the stairs instead of the elevator, I *can't* have three margaritas with dinner every night. And we don't like rules. This is the land of rebellion, after all. This is the land of Paul Revere and James Dean.

But here's a secret, all you mavericks: A budget is your ticket to freedom. It's not really about restrictions and rules; it's about *you* deciding what to do and when to do it. And when you're in charge of your money—the getting, spending, and saving of it—you will be free.

So, how do you make a budget? It's easy to create and stick to a budget, but it's easier not to. Your first step, then, is to commit to the process, which means figuring out why you want and need a budget. Write down all of the reasons to create a budget and all of the reasons not to. Be honest with yourself and write down everything that comes to mind.

| Reasons to Budget | Reasons Not to Budget |
|---|---|
| I want to know where my money goes | It might cut into my clothes/gambling/gear collecting habit |
| I work hard and want to keep more of the money I earn | I might miss the last-chance-only-happens-once-every-two-weeks sale |
| I want to buy a house | Retirement is for the weak! |
| I want to travel more | I'll have to live on thin gruel and watered-down coffee, I'll start wearing plastic bags instead of rain gear, I'll stop brushing my teeth, my girlfriend will break up with me... |
| I want an emergency fund | I'll become one of those weird people who reviews bank statements |
| I want to retire by the time I'm.... | People might think... |

Once you've made the commitment, creating a budget is pretty easy (though expect it to take some time). Here are the four steps to budgeting:

## Know your income

Quick! How much do you make before taxes? After taxes? How much do you contribute to savings or retirement? If you don't have answers to these three questions, get them. And if you do have an answer to that last question but it's something along the lines of, "Savings? What savings?" or, "Retirement is too far off to think about!" please consider the following:

You need to pay yourself first. Financial experts, life coaches, and investment gurus all advise you put 10% of your monthly gross income into savings or retirement right away—before you have a chance to spend it.

The younger you are the more you should be thinking about retirement, because now is the time you can make a huge difference in when and how you retire. See Chapter 6 for details.

## Track your spending

For at least one week, write down *every* expense. Carry around a notepad and pen and jot down all purchases—every sandwich, pack of gum, tip, ATM fee, *every little thing*. To keep it simple, when you record the amounts, always round up. If you space out and forget to note an expense, don't worry. Guesstimate the missing amount at the end of the day and write it down then. Note: you might find it easier to carry around an envelope and collect receipts for every purchase you make throughout the day; then, in the evening, you can sit down and write them out. This method works just as well as the little-notebook-and-pen method, but be advised: the barista might roll his eyes if you ask him to write out a receipt for the 25-cent tip you plunked into the jar.

**Example of daily spending log**

| | |
|---|---|
| Coffee & Muffin | $3.15 |
| Newspaper | $1.00 |
| Parking | $6.15 |
| Movie ticket | $9.00 |
| Popcorn | $3.00 |

## Example of monthy worksheet

### FOOD

| | |
|---|---|
| Dining out: | $ 35 |
| | $ 15 |
| | $ 9 |
| | $ 12 |
| TOTAL: | $ 71 |
| Groceries: | $ 55 |
| | $ 8 |
| | $ 22 |
| | $ 12 |
| | $ 37 |
| TOTAL: | $134 |

### TRANSPORTATION

| | |
|---|---|
| Gas: | $ 45 |
| Parking: | $ 20 |

## Find out where your money goes

The second step is to categorize and tally your monthly spending. The most common major categories are Housing, Food, Utilities, Debt, Insurance, Transportation, Entertainment, Personal, and Retirement/Savings. You will also want to create some subcategories in order to get a more precise picture of your spending patterns. For instance, Food should include the subcategories Groceries and Dining Out. Debt might include the subcategories Student Loan, Credit Cards, and Parents.

Write out your expense categories and subcategories, leaving adequate space under each heading to record your actual expenses. Now, using your bank statement, credit card statements, and the information you gathered while tracking your daily spending, write down every expenditure in the appropriate category. Remember to multiply the incidental expenses you tracked over the week by four, as now you're building a *monthly* record.

## Fixed Expenses vs. Variable Expenses

**Fixed Expenses** occur regularly and are generally the same amount. Some fixed expenses are monthly (rent, fitness club dues), and others are annual or quarterly (car insurance, some utilities). For the latter, figure out how much per month you need to put aside (for instance, if you pay $1,000 for car insurance once a year, you should budget $84 a month; that way, when the bill is due you'll be ready to pay).

**Variable Expenses** vary in frequency and amount. Dining, entertainment, fuel, and clothing are all examples of variable expenses. You have much more control over variable expenses and they can fluctuate more than fixed expenses, so it can be difficult to know what to budget for them. Review your bank and credit card statements—as well as your daily spending notebook—to determine an average of your spending in these categories.

This information easily translates into your first **income statement**:

| INCOME STATEMENT | |
|---|---|
| Monthly Income | $ |
| Minus Monthly Fixed Expenses | – $ |
| Minus Yearly Fixed Expenses (Monthly Average) | – $ |
| Minus Monthly Variable Expenses | – $ |
| Equals Remaining Income | = $ |

Once you have a picture of how you have been getting, saving, and spending your money, decide what you want to do about it in the future. Then write it down to ensure you'll stick to it.

## Fix the leaks!

Is your money leaking away, deflating your wallet along with your future spending choices?

As you review your spending leaks, it will probably become obvious what you need to do to fix them. The trick is to do just that and to do it as soon as possible so you can avoid letting your hard-earned money dribble away. Here are some quick fixes once you recognize the leaks:

**Pay attention.** Know what you're spending, when you're spending it, and why you're spending it. Also, pay attention to the rates you're paying for credit card interest, services, and other variable expenses. If you regularly get stuck with a late payment charge on a bill, write a reminder on the calendar or just pay the bill the day it comes in the mail.

**Common Money Leaks**  *TIP*

- Daily nonessentials (see "The Real Cost of that Latte")
- Fees (most common: using another bank's ATM, late fees for bills)
- High-interest credit cards
- Unused memberships, services, and subscriptions
- Communication services and devices (cell phones, computer access, etc.)
- Convenience items

**Take stock of all the expenses in your life, no matter how minor.** Do you use the online photo membership that pulls $4.95 from your account automatically every month? Do you need that subscription to the newspaper or could you get your news online? Do you regularly go to the gas station that charges 5 cents more per gallon because the cheaper one is on the other side of the street? Little changes can make a big impact. Even if these quick fixes won't make you an instant millionaire, isn't it nice to know that you'll end up keeping more of the money you earn?

**Consider the real price of convenience.** You're a busy person. But convenience spending might mean that you're working double time for the benefit of the drycleaner, the take-out teriyaki shop, and the parking garage owner. It might save you five minutes to use the other bank's ATM, but that time savings could cost you $3—or more!

Now you know the ins and outs of budgeting and are as prepared as anybody to manage your money wisely. However, there's one more thing to keep in mind as you begin the process: The way you think about and deal with money is ultimately a habit. And as with any other habit, altering your approach to your personal finances may entail trials and backslides. If "We all need some retail therapy" or "Spend it when you get it" have been your money mantras for years, you'll find them slipping into your consciousness, guiding your cursor to the "Buy Now!" button. Patience. Think up some new mantras—how about "Keep it 'cause you earn it"—and revisit this chapter often to help you *keep* a grip on your finances.

## The Real Cost of That Latte
### (or Soda, or Bottled Water, or Pack of Gum...)

**What would you do if you won $1,000 on the local radio station giveaway? Shriek? Pump your fist in the air? Well, get ready to jump up and down on the sofa, because you're about to win $1,000 or more!**

Look at your little daily nonessential expenses. A latte here, a smoothie there, a pack of gum, the latest issue of a magazine... If you cut this spending by just $3 a day, you will save $1,095 in a year, $5,475 in 5 years, and over $20,000 in 20 years! Now, if you go beyond saving and invest that $3 a day, the numbers look even better (and the latte looks even less appealing). At a conservative rate of return, you'd have over $26,000 in 15 years and a whopping $43,650 in 20 years.

**You already have the money, now you need to keep more of it.**
(Feel free to shriek and pump your fist in the air the next time you pass that cool, jazz-infused, well-lit coffee shop without spending your money there.)

Online calculators: www.finishrich.com

# LIVE CHEAPLY

## CHAPTER 3

The quick version of this chapter goes something like this: Move back in with your folks. Shop less. Eat in. Save more. Easy enough, you say, but what to wear? The answer is, "neutrals."

See, we all pretty much know the basics of how to live cheaply, so why is it so hard to suck it up for a few years, then revel in accumulated wealth in the not-so-distant future? The problem is that conventional wisdom is often drowned out by the siren song of popular culture, advertising, and easy credit: "Here it is! You want it? You got it!" After all, without these forces, who would have guessed that people look so cute with little dogs? Or that little dogs look so cute in rhinestone-studded collars, bedded in pink fluffy beds, gnawing on teeny organic doggie biscuits? Or that the whole package—dog, collar, bed, biscuits—can be purchased now and paid for later? Celebrities—who can easily afford the whole shebang—make it look not just easy but necessary.

Now, most of us aren't so easily swayed that we'll go out and buy a schnauzer just because our favorite reality TV star has one. But the twin influences of media and easy access to "money" have undeniably put their stamp on our culture. "I want" becomes "I need" becomes "I need it now." Resist the siren song and you'll be miles ahead of the pack, vacationing in Ibiza while some poor soul is paying off ten-year-old credit card bills.

The future beckons, but for now here's how to make the most of the present.

## Find affordable housing

The first step to living cheaply is to find cheap housing. A bachelor pad in downtown Seattle—or San Francisco or Atlanta or Chicago—is perfect for entertaining new friends and decorating with sleek laminate furniture from Sweden. However, such a lifestyle can eat up your earnings faster than you can say, "Let's go back to my place and look at the skyline." Housing takes a 25% - 40% bite out of most people's income, and even more if they live alone in a metropolitan area.

Have you checked out Nebraska lately? How about that recently-converted rec room in your parents' house? OK, OK, if those options are unrealistic, how about seriously reconsidering your oath to "Never have a roommate again as long as I live!" Sure, there are limitations to living back at home or with roommates, but imagine how much money you could save! You could pay down debts, invest, build a nest egg...

## Fake yourself out

Live like you're poor (or, poorer than you are) and you'll get rich; live like you're rich (or, richer than you are) and you'll get poor. In other words, live below your

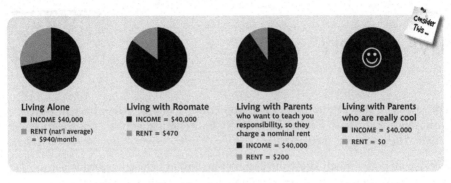

**Living Alone**
- INCOME $40,000
- RENT (nat'l average) = $940/month

**Living with Roomate**
- INCOME = $40,000
- RENT = $470

**Living with Parents**
who want to teach you responsibility, so they charge a nominal rent
- INCOME = $40,000
- RENT = $200

**Living with Parents**
who are really cool
- INCOME = $40,000
- RENT = $0

means. You can fake yourself out by directing, as most financial experts suggest, 10% of your gross income into savings and investments (or paying off debt) before you even lay eyes on it. Pay yourself first. (See Chapter 2.)

## TIP Bring Back Cash!

Cash seems almost quaint these days, little green bills with pictures of old men on them, little jingly coins that go in those funny phones in the glass booths. But maybe it's time to go retro. Study after study has shown that when you pay with cash you spend less; when you pay with debit or credit cards, you spend more. The Wall Street Journal reported that card companies see the average transaction at McDonald's jump from $4.50 to $7 when customers use debit or credit instead of cash. It's the difference between spending money and spending "money."

## Eat in more often

Food accounts for 10% of a person's income, according to the United States Department of Agriculture. Because it's a variable expense it's a great place to "tighten the belt." The best ways to trim your food budget:

**Eat at home as often as possible.** If eating is a big part of your social scene, do more dinners at home with friends.

**When you do eat out, remember that restaurants love it when you order drinks, desserts, and appetizers.** Avoid these extras. They usually have the biggest profit margins and really pad your bill. (For the price of one soda, you can buy a six-pack at the grocery store.)

**Shop the perimeter of the grocery store.** Once you go into the aisles, your grocery bill expands like a pair of elastic-waist jeans.

**Buy store brands.** Often, store brands are manufactured by the same folks who make the name-brand stuff. Even when they're not, the substantial savings you get with the store-brand products will make you forget any taste difference.

**Buy in bulk.** Sometimes. If it makes sense for your lifestyle. Do you drink gallons of coffee a week? Then buy it in bulk. One caution about the mega-warehouse-super stores: It's easy to get distracted and talk yourself into overbuying because everything seems like such a good deal.

## Be a cheaper date

There's lots of fun to be had for very little money. Check online or in your local newspaper for bargain movies, eats, and other date ideas. Two habits to nix if you have them: Shopping for entertainment, and buying rounds of drinks.

## Shop smart

Because clothing generally accounts for 5% of a person's budget, it's worth including here. It is a variable expense that some of us find hard to control. Here's how to keep your clothing appetite in check:

**Buy clothes at the end of the season or in the thick of the season.** The $300 jacket you saw in October will be $120 in December.

**Shop for staples**—t-shirts, underwear, socks—at an inexpensive retailer.

**Fill your wardrobe with black and neutrals**; this will allow you to mix and match most of your outfits and they'll all look fresh and chic.

**Shop second hand.** It's an easy way to be creative on a budget. You can find trendy, unique, and often high-quality pieces at thrift stores and consignment shops.

### Four Easy Non-Spending Habits

- **Ask yourself,** "Is this necessary?" By asking yourself if you really need something, you will be forced to pay attention to what you're spending and why.
- **Say no to add-ons.** Extra insurance, the "deluxe" car wash, dessert...there are innumerable opportunities to "super size" your expenses. Recognize and avoid them.
- **Spend nothing day.** Designate one day a week—or a month—a "Spend Nothing Day." Not only will you save money on the designated day, but it will help you see how much and how frequently you spend on the other days.
- **Cool down.** Give yourself at least 24 hours to think about any purchases over $100. Also, take an item back if you get home and realize it isn't something you really, really want or need.

**So that's it:** the quick and the not-so-quick versions of how to live cheaply. If you want to get truly frugal you can visit websites dedicated to really stretching dollars (Create rubber bands by cutting up used latex gloves! Make wrapping paper out of old junk mail!). However, you don't necessarily need to radically alter your lifestyle in order to keep more money and spend less. Make a few adjustments at a time and pretty soon you'll be so distracted by your swelling bank account that you won't notice you're picking up dates in your parents' minivan.

**SOURCES**

www.ers.usda.gov/AmberWaves/September08/Findings/PercentofIncome.htm

www.washingtonpost.com/wp-srv/business/personalfinance/gradbudgetcalculator.htm

## CHAPTER 4

# READ THIS CHAPTER EVEN THOUGH IT'S ABOUT INSURANCE

Insurance is like a GPS unit: when conditions are good, you don't have to think about it and when conditions are bad you're glad you have it. Plus it looks gadgety and cool. Scratch that. Insurance has, in fact, nothing to do with anything that is fun or interesting or gadgety or cool. Insurance at its best is dull…until you have to make a claim. Then it's absolutely necessary.

Even if you're broke, young, healthy, cool, and really careful? Yes, you still need insurance, but the difference between you and those of us who write this kind of advice is that when *you* make payments to the insurance company, you can console yourself by saying, "At least I'm still young, healthy and cool!" And that's worth something.

**Good To Know**

**As a recent college graduate, you probably need four or five types of insurance. These include:**

- Auto Insurance
- Health Insurance
- Life Insurance
- Home Owners / Renter's Insurance
- Disability Insurance

But let's address the other part of the above scenario—the making payments part. It's not pleasant to pay for insurance, no matter your age or financial status. When all goes well, after all, you don't need it. It's understandable that some people see insurance payments as self-imposed hardship or proof of having been suckered into some silly deal. But you are definitely not a sucker.

You are, in fact, a well-informed (if, possibly, slightly broke) consumer—who can find appropriate, affordable insurance coverage. The real hardship comes from not having the right insurance coverage when you need it. Read on to find out more.

## Health insurance

This is a must. Even if you are young and healthy, it is an enormous risk to go without health coverage. Taking such a risk—even for a few months—could have devastating consequences. The out-of-pocket cost of a broken leg is over $2,000. And if you need surgery for that broken leg, you can add an additional $17,000 to over $33,000. Going to the ER for a sore throat, getting tested, and being told to go home and get some rest will run you about $500. (Of course, avoiding the ER when you *do* have a serious illness can cost even more.) And these examples are small potatoes next to catastrophic illnesses, which can easily rack up tens and hundreds of thousands of dollars.

Despite these alarming facts, young adults have historically been inclined to take a gamble and go without health insurance. In fact, 18 to 24 year olds are the least likely of any age group to have health insurance; Over 30% of people in this age bracket are uninsured. However, recent legislation may change that statistic. Under the 2010 Affordable Care Act, children may stay on their parents' health plan until age 26. Prior to the Affordable Care Act, some insurance providers allowed children to stay on their parents' plans, but many stopped coverage as early as age 19 or upon graduation. (Note: in some states you may be eligible to remain on your parents' plan past the age of 26.)

Many college students rely on their parents' policy for as long as possible, or sign on to their university plan, which is relatively inexpensive. When graduates have to transition—from their parents' plan or the university plan—they suddenly face a gap in coverage that may seem too expensive or too trivial to bridge. It's an understandable response when you're young, healthy and broke. But stuff happens and it tends to happen when it's least convenient or foreseeable. Here are some options to help you stay insured through this life transition:

**KEY VOCABULARY: A Quick Primer on Insurance Terms**

**Premium:** The fee you pay, usually assessed annually or semiannually

**Deductible:** The amount of money you have to pay on a claim before the insurance kicks in. A higher deductible means a lower premium.

**Rider:** A provision attached to a policy that adds to or changes the original policy.

**COBRA**: COBRA (Consolidated Omnibus Budget Reconciliation Act) guarantees that workers can maintain their health insurance when they leave or lose a job, and it also applies to young adults who lose the coverage of their parents' plan. If you've been covered under your parents' policy, you can keep that coverage for at least 18 months—if you pay the premiums. Not cheap, but it keeps you covered.

**Federal or state insurance exchange:** As of 2013, individuals may purchase affordable health care through state or federal health care exchanges. These online marketplaces offer side-by-side comparisons of various plans for comprehensive health insurance. People who make under a certain amount qualify for tax credit subsidies. Go to www.healthcare.gov to find out what's available to you.

**University Health Plan**: If you have been participating in your college's health care plan, you can extend this coverage as well. You'll get to keep your doctors, but you will have to pay higher premiums and the coverage usually only lasts a few months.

**Short-Term Policy**: Cheaper than the other options—and higher risk—these policies generally cover one to six months. Designed to cover unexpected events, but don't usually cover preventative healthcare or pre-existing conditions.

**Catastrophic Policy**: The name says a lot. This bare-bones coverage generally pays for hospital stays. Not doctors' fees, but the cost of room and food while you're hospitalized.

Health insurance is expensive, but not having it can be financially devastating. Choose a plan that makes sense for your lifestyle. A short-term policy might work very well for someone who is in excellent health and needs coverage for just a couple of months; however, someone who has a family or personal history of illness or who foresees a longer gap in coverage should probably opt to pay a little more in order to get good preventative care.

## Health care plans

It used to be that if you got sick you could just send your brother for a doctor. He would ride for four days across the frozen plain to bring the local doctor right to your bedside. Sure, there might be leeches and bloodletting involved, but you'd get personalized service and you could pay for it with eggs, pickles, and cords of wood! By comparison, health care today is sterile and complicated. (However, life expectancy is up by a few decades, so there's a trade-off.)

The **fee-for-service insurance plan** most closely resembles the personalized service of the days of yore (minus the bloodletting, of course). With this type of plan, you can choose any doctor and any hospital you want, and the insurance company pays between 80 to 100 percent of the expense. What's the catch? Fee-for-service plans are generally *very* expensive.

Most people now are covered by managed-care plans instead. Here are descriptions of the most common managed-care health insurance models:

**Health Maintenance Organizations (HMOs):** HMOs provide health care through a network of doctors, hospitals, and medical professionals. Participants and/or their employers pay a monthly premium in exchange for the HMO's comprehensive care. Participants must seek care from network primary care physicians (PCPs) and must have a PCP referral in order to see a specialist.

## At a Glance: Compare Health Insurance Plans    *GooD To KNow*

|  | Overall Flexibility | Overall Cost | Choice of Physician | Easy Access to Specialists | Premiums | Deductibles | Co-Payments | Out-of-Pocket expenses | Paperwork (reimbursement forms) |
|---|---|---|---|---|---|---|---|---|---|
| **HMO** | Low | Low | Within network only | Need referral | Low | None | Low | Low | Low |
| **POS (Hybrid)** | Moderate | Low - Moderate | Within network encouraged | Need referral | Low-Moderate | None | Low (except for non-network care) | Low | Moderate |
| **PPO** | Moderate-High | Moderate-High | Within network encouraged | Yes | Moderate-high | Moderate | N/A | Moderate-High | High |
| **Fee-For-Service** | High | High | Yes | Yes | High | High | N/A | High | High |

**Preferred Provider Organizations (PPOs):** PPOs have a network of preferred healthcare providers, but participants may elect to seek care from a physician outside the network if they are willing to pay more. Unlike HMOs, PPOs generally allow participants to access specialists without a referral.

**Hybrid, or Point-Of-Service (POS) Plans:** POSs allow participants to see providers outside the preferred provider network (like PPOs) for a slightly higher co-payment or deductible, but they require participants to select a primary care physician (like HMOs).

## Flexible Spending Accounts (FSAs)
Finally! An acronym that can save you some money! An FSA lets you pay for your health care over the course of the year—with before-tax dollars. This lowers your taxable salary and can save you over $1,000 a year.

First, estimate how much you'll spend in a year on health care—consider the costs of co-payments, office visits, and prescriptions. Next, through your employer and an FSA coordinator, contribute a portion of your paycheck to your FSA. Finally, document and report health-related expenses to the FSA, which will reimburse you. As you can see, it's not a difficult process but it's one that trips some people up. Remember to estimate your expenses carefully at the beginning of the year; you're only allowed to carry over $500 from one year to the next. Also, hold on to all those receipts and other documentation of health care expenses, as you'll need to itemize them in order to get full reimbursement. Note: *There is a $2500 limit for FSA contributions.*

## Renter's insurance
While health insurance involves endless terms, acronyms, what-ifs, and a not insignificant portion of your salary, renter's insurance is simple: Protect your stuff for cheap. You can get a good policy for as low as $100 a year. A paltry fee for a lot of peace of mind.

What's covered? Damage to or loss of your computer, MP3 player, other electronics, sports equipment, clothing, and furniture. (Remember: If you apartment is burgled or burned or mold-infested, your landlord is not responsible for your stuff.) These policies even cover your belongings when you're in transition (moving across country, for instance). And if you have irreplaceable objects—jewelry, original artwork, antiques, LPs—you can pay a little more and add a rider for them to your policy.

Another important aspect to renter's insurance is liability coverage. It covers you for lawsuits if someone falls and hurts him or herself at your place, if an appliance overheats and starts a fire, or if your cute dog bites a visitor.

## Auto insurance

If you have a car, you must have auto insurance. "Must," as in "are legally required to," at least in most places. Almost all states require car owners to have automobile liability insurance. Despite these laws, there are plenty of uninsured drivers anyway, which is another reason for *you* to have complete coverage. Insurance, after all, is really about your financial protection. An auto accident can wipe out the uninsured in more ways than one, leaving a person vulnerable to lawsuits and staggering hospital bills.

Following are the major categories of automobile insurance. The first four are highly recommended and/or legally required, depending on your state:

**Bodily Injury Liability:** If you injure someone, this component of your insurance covers the injured party's medical costs. Most states require that motorists have some bodily injury coverage. Your insurance agent can tell you what that minimum is. It's also a good idea to increase your coverage in this area as your assets grow; the more you have the more you can be sued for and the more liability coverage you need.

**Property Damage Liability:** This covers the costs to repair or replace damaged property—other vehicles, roadway signs and structures, buildings, etc. This is not always a legal responsibility, but it's an important aspect to financial protection.

**Medical Payments or Personal Injury Protection (PIP):** This covers medical expenses of the driver and passengers, regardless of who is at fault. It also covers injuries you may suffer when riding in or driving another person's car.

**Uninsured/Underinsured Motorist Liability:** An estimated 16% of drivers on the road do not have insurance or have inadequate coverage. So if one of them slams into your car, you need to have some way of paying for repairs to you and the car. This component of your auto insurance will cover lost wages, medical expenses, and property damage resulting from a run-in with an uninsured motorist.

The following categories are not necessary for every driver. If you drive a junker with missing floorboards, mushrooms in the upholstery, and bumper stickers keeping the doors from falling off, you can probably forego collision and comprehensive coverage. However, if you're still making payments, your lender might require these.

### Deciphering Insurance Policies

*As you start researching insurance policies, you'll notice they format coverage like this:*

100/300/50. What do these numbers mean? The first one refers to bodily injury coverage per person, the second one refers to bodily injury coverage per accident, and the third one refers to coverage for property damage. You can raise or lower your coverage in these categories according to your personal situation, as long as you maintain the minimum amount required by law in your state.

## Tips for Controlling the Cost of Auto Insurance

1. **Shop around to compare prices and coverage,** but remember that cheaper can cost you more in the long run. You want to know if you can afford the premiums and what kind of service and coverage you'll actually get if you end up in an accident. Check the Better Business Bureau (www.bbb.org) to learn more about a company's track record.

2. **Remember: Premium up, deductible down.** Deductible up, premium down. If your finances could weather a higher deductible, you probably want to opt for a lower premium.

3. **Calculate the cost of insurance before you buy a car.** Some cars cost more to insure, either because they're simply more expensive, or speedier, or more likely to get jacked.

4. **Drive less, pay less.** Your mileage is included in insurance calculations, so if you choose public transportation for commuting rather than your car, you'll pay less for coverage.

5. **Keep your record clean.** Of course, DUIs, DWIs, and other traffic violations will raise your rates considerably.

6. **Ask about other ways to lower your insurance.** If you have airbags, park in a garage, have an alarm, and take a defensive driving course, for instance, you could find yourself with a very pleasing premium. Also ask about discounts if you consolidate all your insurance needs with one provider.

**Collision:** Covers damage to your car caused by an automobile accident, whether or not you are at fault.

**Comprehensive:** Covers non-collision damage, such as vandalism, hail dents, and tree damage.

One common question related to auto insurance is, "Do I need to purchase insurance when I rent a car?" The answer is maybe. If your own insurance policy does not have collision or comprehensive, then you should accept the rental agency's plan. If your policy does include collision or comprehensive, it should cover you when you're driving a rental, but it's always a good idea to double check with them before you're standing at the rental car company counter. Also, if you are paying for the rental car with a credit card, check with your credit card company about coverage. Many credit card providers offer Collision Damage Waiver coverage as a benefit to cardholders.

**Love the Blue Book, Hate the Blue Book.** Type in "blue book" on your favorite search engine and you'll come up with sites that contain charts of the fair market value of automobiles (Kelley Blue Book and Nada Guides are two such guides). You'll love knowing the fair market value when you're purchasing a used car, as that magic number can give you the leverage you need to talk a salesperson down in price. However, when it comes to insurance, the blue book value can leave you feeling a little deflated. A car you absolutely love—maybe a first car, one you've driven cross country, one that's seen you through great dates and break-ups, one you've even *named*— well, according to the blue book it's worth $390. And that's the amount of the check from the insurance company that will "cover" the loss of the car if it's totaled. Sigh.

## Insurance you don't need

You've heard a lot about what you must have, should have, need to get. Now we're going to tell you what you might not need and definitely don't want. Insurance is for stuff that matters—your health and your financial well-being. It is not for little stuff, like MP3 players or TVs. Here's a short list of what you can probably pass on:

**Extended Warranty and Repair Plans**—The nice salesperson has spent a lot of time convincing you whatever he or she is selling is a great product. Well, then, it doesn't need "insurance." Say no. Even if it breaks, you'll come out ahead.

**Home Warranty Plans**—Accept a home warranty if it's already part of the selling package, but don't pay to tack one on. Hire a really thorough home inspector with the money you save to make sure the house you're buying is sound.

**Credit Life and Credit Disability Policies**—These show up as offers in your bank and credit card statements. They are fairly inexpensive, but the corresponding benefits are low, too. If you have life insurance or disability insurance, these credit policies are especially redundant.

Your individual insurance needs depend on a variety of factors. Before you set out to purchase insurance, arm yourself with knowledge: Read up, check with other sources, and know what you want to get into. The more you know the better coverage you'll have and the more money you'll save.

**SOURCES**
www.hhs.gov/ociio/regulations/adult_child_fact_sheet.html
www.costhelper.com/cost/health/broken-leg.html
healthreform.kff.org/timeline.aspx
**Uninsured drivers:** www.npr.org/templates/story/story.php?storyId=99712452

## CHAPTER 5

# PLAN FOR EMERGENCIES

Worst-case scenarios don't make great dinner conversation. "Think about it: you could get fired, just like that, and be out of work for, like, months! And have you given much thought to flesh-eating bacteria? Did you know you could get it from the teeniest little cut? Pass the salsa, will you?" In fact, a lot of us, when someone brings up the unthinkable, do the equivalent of a child's response to something she doesn't want to hear: We plug our ears and sing, "La! La! Not listening! Not listening!"

> **Consider This —**
> **Did you know?**
> The average length of unemployment in the United States in the first half of 2013 was over **7 months**—an increase in the 3 – 5 month average length of unemployment in the years 2000 – 2010. Source: Bureau of Labor Statistics

We don't have to get morbid here, but it's worth unplugging the ears for a minute to acknowledge that, yes, bad stuff happens. Accidents, medical emergencies, unexpected unemployment—they are unpredictable, sometimes frightening, and definitely part of every person's life. We don't know everything that we'll face in our lives, but we can prepare financially so that if and when something happens, we'll be as ready as possible.

Everybody needs some kind of emergency fund that can cover their expenses for a while if they find themselves incapacitated, unemployed, or simply faced with a knock-out expense. Nobody expects the busted transmission or Sunday morning plumbing emergency. People without the means to keep themselves financially afloat after disaster strikes often find themselves awash in credit card debt.

Do you know how expensive a root canal at 18% interest is? Let's just say that at least in the dentist's chair you get painkillers. When you're home three years later making another payment to your credit card company—now, *that's* pain.

How much you need in your fund, how you'll build it, and where you'll keep it is what this chapter will help you figure out.

## How can I create an emergency fund when I'm broke?
Like most people at your stage of life, you might not be able to afford to contribute a lot right now. It is important to make your future self a priority, however. You *can* begin an emergency fund and we have some tips on how to trick yourself into paying into it without feeling more strapped.

## How much should I keep in my emergency fund?
Financial planners agree that you should have such a fund, but they disagree as to how much you need in it. Most planners, though, say that a person should have between two to six months of their minimum monthly living expenses socked away. At your stage of life it's appropriate to work toward the low end of the spectrum: Aim for building a reserve worth at least two to three months of your minimum living expenses.

## Sample Emergency Fund Plan

To figure out how much you need, add up your minimum monthly expenses. Only include real necessities.

| | |
|---|---|
| Rent | $850 |
| Food | $250 |
| Health Insurance | $200 |
| Utilities | $80 |
| Transportation | $95 |
| Monthly Total | $1,475 |
| Emergency Fund (for 3 months) | $4,425 |

# How can I build an emergency fund?

Once you figure out how much you need, you can create monthly payments for yourself. Calculate your projected total, then break that into manageable monthly payments. On the first of every month, for instance, write a $100 check to your emergency account. Or, better yet, arrange to have it automatically transferred. (People are much more likely to contribute consistently to a savings or retirement account if they do it as soon as—or before!—their paycheck hits their checking account. You really won't notice these deductions until you need to call on them.) At $100 a month, it will take you about three and a half years to create a $4,000 reserve. Sure, it's the tortoise approach, but you need to sustain the contributions. Pace yourself. If you're certain you can contribute more, however, go for it. If you've looked over your budget and can only afford $50, do it. Some is better than none. In fact, put a little sum in an account *right now*, then you can read the rest of this chapter knowing you've got a head start.

# Where should I keep my emergency fund?

That's a really good question. There are two general rules about placing your emergency money:

1. **You need to be able to access the funds quickly, but not too quickly.** Do choose a bank and account type that makes it easy for you to deposit funds on a regular basis. Do not put these funds into your regular savings account, especially if it's linked to your checking account. That will make it too easy for you to tap into if you have an "emergency" urge to buy a great pair of shoes or need an "emergency" night out on the town. Some people set up accounts in a bank across town or one that doesn't have a lot of ATMs available, just so they can reduce access (and temptation). Also, it's not a good idea to put your emergency funds into stocks, as they're higher risk and usually harder to cash out.

2. **Your money should be earning interest (let it work while you work).** If you keep it in your coin jar or under your mattress, your money will just lose value. Inflation in the past decade has hovered around 3%. That means that $1,000 tucked under a mattress will only be worth about $970 in a year. You want your hard-earned money to keep up with—or, preferably, outpace—inflation. (Note that many savings accounts do not offer a return higher than the rate of inflation.) Check out high-interest savings accounts, money market accounts (MMA), certificates of deposits (CDs), and bonds.

There are enough unpredictables in life—but your finances are, to a very large extent, within your control. The truth is that imagining worst-case scenarios may not be great conversation, but thinking about the what-ifs can help you establish financial priorities and put those priorities into action. Ultimately you will reduce anxiety in your life.

## Tips For Growing Your Emergency Fund

**Adopt a couple of these habits and you'll be surprised at how quickly your reserve grows (and how little you notice your contributions).**

1. **Coin jar.** Treat coins as decorative objects rather than currency; never use them to actually pay for anything. Up the ante by using cash frequently (instead of your debit card), which will give you even more opportunities to feed that coin jar.

2. **Halve your gift money.** Does grandma still send you birthday checks? Imagine her delight when your thank-you card tells her how much you enjoyed spending half on a little birthday treat for yourself and depositing half into savings! There's more than one way to treat yourself, after all.

3. **Get physical.** Tie a monetary reward to another personal goal. For instance, if you've resolved to work out four times a week, make a "tip jar" that you can feed every time you actually do work out. Add $1 each time and you'll be able to see your progress toward both goals—by the end of the year you'll have over $200 and rock hard abs.

4. **Break a habit to make a habit.** Do you have a frivolous expense habit? Something that you purchase on a regular basis that leaks money? Take a break from the habit and put the difference you save into your emergency fund. Instead of purchasing a new paperback, check it out at the library. Ka-ching! You can deposit $12.99. Go from eating out four times a week to two. You'll save money by eating at home, and you can deposit the rest.

5. **Keep paying retired bills.** Did you pay your car off? Awesome. If you're used to a $250 per month expense like a car payment, you can keep it up—but this time give it to yourself. Same goes for utility bills, which often vary seasonally. If your electric bill is high in the winter and low in the summer, you can budget for the high bills and pay yourself the difference in those warmer months.

6. **Tax refund.** Chances are pretty good that you will receive a tax refund the first couple years after graduation. Avoid the temptation to spend it. Instead, make a nice contribution to your emergency fund.

6. **Round up.** Many banks now offer a free service that rounds up any purchases you make to the next dollar, then deposits that amount in your savings account. For instance, if you pay a $32.30 bill at a restaurant on your debit card, the transaction will be recorded as $33. (The restaurant will get its $32.30 and your savings account will get 70 cents.) This is a painless way to build up your savings—and you'll be amazed at how much the change adds up!

## Emergency Fund Accounts

Here are the questions to ask when searching for the right place for your emergency money:

- Is the account FDIC insured?
- How much interest will it earn?
- Does it require a minimum opening amount?
- Does it require a minimum balance?
- Does your money need to be in the account for a certain amount of time?
- Are there any fees associated with the account?

Note that one account might be best when you're starting out, but another will be a better choice in a year, as you accrue more money. You might begin by putting money into a high-interest savings account because you can access it quickly. After twelve months, you can transfer it to a long-term CD that earns even more interest, and build up the savings account again.

# THOUGHT ABOUT RETIREMENT?

## CHAPTER 6

This topic is pretty important, so it's fitting here to turn to ancient wisdom. More specifically, to the ancient wisdom of Lao Tzu, who said in his great text *The Way of Lao Tzu*, "A journey of a thousand miles begins with a single step." Now, Lao Tzu died thousands of years ago, so we'll never know what he would have said about compounding interest and Roth IRAs, but one can speculate he'd have this advice about retirement in general: "立即开始为退休储蓄!" (Or: "Start that thing now, baby!")

To which you might understandably reply, "But, Lao Tzu, sir, teacher, I am young and poor and retirement is a distant land for old people who wear wrinkle-free pants and talk about fiber all the time. What have I to do with that?" To which he might (understandably) shake his head and pull out a scroll or a spreadsheet or a chart that looks something like this:

Think about this for a second: Invest $1,000 when you're 25 and it will grow (this chart assumes your money earns a conservative 8% interest) to $21,725 by the time you're 65!

Now, wait five years and invest the $1,000 when you're 30 and your money still grows, but at age 65 you'll have $14, 785, quite a chunk of change for a $1,000 investment, but substantially less than if you had invested it when you were younger.

## Consider This ...

### How Much do You Have to Work to Earn $20,000?

How many hours does it take you to make that much money? How much sweat? How much anxiety? How many meetings? By contrast, your hypothetical invested $1,000 does *nothing* and earns you the same amount. Like an overpaid, injured athlete on steroids, your money sits on the sidelines and grows and grows.

| Starting at age 25, invest this per month... | And, at 8% compounded interest, you'll have **this** by age 65... |
| --- | --- |
| $100 | $349,000 |
| $200 | $698,000 |
| $300 | $1,000,000 |

Want to plug in your own numbers? There are many compound interest calculators online. Check out the National Council on Economic Education's interactive calculator at www.econedlink.org.

And that's the key: You are young now. The best time to invest in your retirement is now. You may or may not have much money to put aside for retirement, but you have time. Compound interest will make even a modest monthly investment a substantial retirement fund. Imagine yourself thirty-five or forty years now (or even fifteen years from now, if you're really serious about preparing for an early retirement): What would you say to your younger, just-graduated-from-college self? Would you regret contributing to a retirement account? Would you regret not contributing to one?

The destination is an enjoyable, fruitful, anxiety-free retirement and, whether yours will be one of wrinkle-free pants or surf shorts, the single step that begins the journey is investing in a retirement account. The earlier, the better.

## Who Will Pay for Your Retirement?

You. The good news is that you will live a longer, healthier life than your predecessors. There really is no bad news, but if you want a comfortable, worry-free retirement it up to you, and you alone. Your grandparents' generation had pensions and Social Security and, because of shorter life expectancy, fewer post-working years to provide for. The likelihood that you'll work for a company that offers a pension is very small; that you'll work for that company long enough to earn a worthwhile pension practically nonexistent. Social Security? You'll keep paying into it, but don't expect to get much out of it. Very few retirees today find it enough to live off of. Whatever you get from Uncle Sam should be considered a bonus, absolutely not the basis of your retirement.

## How much money do you need to retire?

The answer to this question is: A lot. What "a lot" means depends on what retirement means to you. Do you want a kayak, Bayliner, or yacht? Do you see yourself taking walks, golfing, or heli-skiing? Think about how young you want to be when you retire, what kind of lifestyle you hope to have in retirement, and calculate from there. Many financial planners recommend you aim for 75% of your annual salary (based on your last few years of employment) available for each year of retirement. This might be a working figure for you, especially if your housing costs are limited by then (if, for example, you've paid off your mortgage by the time you retire). Of course, other variables come into play: What will a dollar be worth when you retire? How much will inflation eat up your retirement earnings? How much will you be paying for healthcare when you reach that age? You will find many online retirement calculators that can help you get started figuring out how much you'll need in order to retire comfortably. A good basic retirement calculator is at www.aarp.org.

## Retirement plan options

There are two broad categories of retirement plans: defined benefit plans and employer-sponsored plans. (We'll cover plans for the self-employed in the next section.)

**Defined benefit plans** are commonly referred to as pension plans, and they used to be the standard: You graduate, find employment with Company Bluechip, work there for 30 years, retire, and Company Bluechip pays you a monthly pension based on a calculation of your years of service and salary. "Defined benefit" is a promise: In exchange for your hard work and loyalty, we will invest on behalf of you and your coworkers, and continue to provide for you in your retirement years.

These plans are not as common now as in your grandparents' generation. Why not? They are expensive for companies to maintain (partly because of those pesky increases in life expectancy!), companies can no longer expect and employees no longer promise long-term loyalty (and, of course, companies are not necessarily loyal to their employees), and the workforce has exerted pressure—especially in bull markets—to command its own investments. Hence, the emphasis now is on employer-sponsored plans.

**Employer-sponsored plans,** also known as defined-contribution plans, include the 401 (k), 403 (b) and 457. (To keep it simple, we'll refer to all these related plans as 401(k).) These plans do not guarantee a set payout amount upon retirement like a pension plan does. Your payout will depend on how much you contributed over the years, if and how much your employer contributed, and how well the investments did. Unlike a pension plan, you have a great deal of control over your account and can decide how much of it to invest in stocks, bonds, and other investments. If your employer offers a retirement plan, you really should take advantage of the opportunity.

Why? It's free money! Impossible, you say. No. Here's how you get free (and legal) money for very little effort:

- **Tax free.** Contributions to defined-benefit plans are tax-free. Your monthly contribution goes into your retirement account before withholding taxes are applied. This lowers your tax bill. And because you are not taxed on the earnings until you take them out, you have lots of years of compounding interest in your favor.

- **Automatically deducted.** Your contributions can be automatically deducted every month, so you don't "feel" the loss.

- **Employer contributions.** Some employers even contribute to the plan. If yours does, make sure you contribute enough to get the highest allowable contribution from your employer. This truly is FREE MONEY and you need to make the most of it.

- **No fees.** Most of these plans involve no fees.

Other things you should know about employer-sponsored plans:

**Employer match option.** Some employers match a certain, stated percentage of your contribution—typically between 50 and 100 percent—up to 6 percent of your annual gross salary. If your employer matches, take it to the limit! Contribute as much as it takes to get their maximum contribution. Yes, this is redundant with the bullet point above, but it's that important. Not convinced? Think about it this way: The average raise is 4%. If your employer matches up to 6%, you are basically getting a 6% raise, tax-free!

**Contribution limits.** In 2011, you can contribute as much as $16,500 pre-tax to your retirement account. That amount is set to adjust for inflation every year, check the IRS's website for the most current contribution limits. (www.irs.gov)

## To Participate or Not to Participate?

Consider This ...

Rachel is 23 and newly employed. She knows that participating in her employer's retirement program is important, but she is trying to save money for a dream vacation. What should she do? Let's just look at her first year of employment.

| OPTION A: | OPTION B: |
|---|---|
| Contribute $1,200 (or $100/month). Leave the contribution in the retirement account until age 60. | Don't contribute the $1,200. Pay taxes (18% federal, 4% state, in this case). |
| **Total: $21,550** | **Total: $940** |

These two options are conservative. Option A could potentially net much more money—if Rachel's employer matched her contributions, she would have more than double the $21,550 by the time she was 60. Also, the account may well earn above 8% interest. Option B, on the other hand, would be even further reduced with other standard deductions.

**Vesting.** Vesting refers to your ownership rights to your retirement money. You are fully vested in your own contributions. Any money you invest into a 401(k) at Company B will be yours when you move on to Company L. However, if your employer provides matching funds, those do not vest until you've proven you're going to stick around for a while. Each company has its own vesting schedule, but it's likely that, after 1 year you'd be partially vested (maybe 10% or so), after 2 years a little more vested (perhaps 20%), and so on. For many companies, you need to hang in for at least 5 years before you can take all the matching funds with you when you go. Be aware of your employer's vesting schedule; if you want to leave the company but it's just a matter of months before you're more fully vested, it might be worth sticking around so that when you do leave you can take more of that free money with you.

**Changing jobs.** When you change jobs you keep everything you've contributed to your retirement account. As we mentioned above, you may or may not get to keep the funds your employer has contributed, but what you have deposited is all yours. So, what do you do with your 401 (k) when you switch to a new employer? Read on to learn the basics of rollovers.

**Rollovers.** This gets really complicated, so we'll just provide an overview here and some good sources where you can learn more about this topic. When you have a 401(k) set up with an employer and then you switch jobs, you have a few options for handling that retirement money.

- You can leave it alone if you're happy with how it's performing at Former Employer, or
- You can transfer it—roll it over—to your 401 (k) at New Employer, or
- You can roll it over to an IRA, or
- You can take the money and run.

That last one sounds tempting, but it's a bad, bad idea. When you withdraw your retirement money early you get taxed, then penalized. Whoosh! You withdraw $1,000 and walk away with about $750 (depending on your tax bracket). That's not even counting all those future potential earnings our friend Lao Tzu laid out for us earlier.

Now, assuming you choose any of the three other ideas—all of them good, except for taking the money out—you need to deal with *how* to roll over that money. If you can avoid touching it, you're going to be in good shape. In other words, if Former Employer cuts you a check, then you transfer that check to your new 401(k) or IRA, you'll encounter withholding taxes. You'll get the money back at tax time, but you may have to fork out of your own pocket to transfer the whole amount or face penalties. And, if you don't perform the rollover within 60 days, you'll have to pay the 10% early withdrawal penalty. In order to avoid any penalties and taxes, you need to avoid touching the money at all by completing what's called a trustee-to-trustee transfer. Your human resource department at your current or new employer can help walk you through this process.

**Withdrawing early.** When you withdraw from your 401(k) you get hit with income tax *and* a 10% penalty. Ouch. There goes all that compounded interest. Do anything you can to avoid touching your retirement until you reach the age 59 ½ (the magical age at which you can begin accessing your retirement funds). Note: under certain circumstances—such as having to pay for the cost of a sudden disability—you might be eligible to withdraw early without having to pay the penalty.

**Borrowing from your retirement.** Many plans allow you to borrow from yourself, but it can be hazardous to your long-term financial health. These loans usually involve fees, operate on a strict and short repayment plan (generally within five years, though if you're borrowing for a down payment on a house you might have more time to pay yourself back), and require you to pay interest as determined by your plan administrator.

## Self-employed and small business plans
If you are self-employed or work for a small business, there are several retirement plan options available to you.

### Simplified Employee Pension (SEP)
A SEP is a type of IRA that is great for someone who is self-employed and has no employees. Yes, only the employer can contribute to the plan, but you are your own employer, right? Therefore, you can contribute up to 25% of your earnings, up to a maximum of $52,000 a year. (These amounts are from the 2013 tax year.) This is deducted off the top of your income (read: tax break!). Some states even allow the deduction from state taxes, too. Warning: Watch your contribution date. The IRS cares.

If you are an employee of a small business that participates in a SEP program, your employer determines your contribution level.

### Savings Incentive Match Plan (SIMPLE)
Businesses with fewer than 100 employees sometimes offer a SIMPLE plan. The key letter in this acronym is "M." Match. Employees with this type of IRA can contribute up to $12,000—tax deferred—annually. (Note: This is the 2013 contribution limit.) Employers must match employee contributions dollar for dollar (up to 3% of annual gross compensation) or contribute 2% of your salary.

### Keogh plans
Also referred to as money-purchase or profit-sharing plans, Keoghs are tax-deferred pension plans for those with self-employment income. They are complicated, paper-intensive, and best used under the supervision of a financial professional.

### Individual Retirement Accounts (IRAs)
If your employer doesn't offer a retirement program—or if you're hooked on saving for retirement and want to sock away even more money—an IRA may be perfect for you. IRAs are, as the name implies, *individually* directed. Whereas an employer's 401(k) plan gives you a range of options within a program, an IRA is your creation. There are two types of IRAs, traditional and Roth.

### Traditional IRA
Like the 401(k), a traditional IRA is tax-deferred—you don't pay taxes until you withdraw the money and in many cases you can deduct what you do contribute. In order to formally set up an IRA, work with a bank, financial planner, or mutual fund company. It's not terribly complicated, but will require precise documentation in order to maintain the tax-deferred status.

Things to know about the traditional IRA:

- **Expect fees.** As with any financial decision, shop around, get advice, and go with a well-respected organization you can trust.

- **Early withdrawal.** Know that early withdrawal entails a 10% penalty (in addition to the taxes due). However, there are some exceptions, including one for people who want to use the money to pay for school and another for first-time homebuyers.

- **Single person options.** If you are single and not participating in an employer-sponsored plan, you can put up to $5,500 a year into your IRA and deduct the full amount on your tax return. If you are single and you do participate in an employer-sponsored plan, you can put up to $5,500 a year into your IRA and deduct the full amount if your adjusted gross income is $59,000 or less (in 2013). If your income is higher, you will have a partial deduction.

- **Married person options.** If you are married, filing jointly, your deduction eligibility depends on your income and whether you and/or your spouse already take part in an employer-sponsored plan. Check with the IRS website or a tax professional to figure out the limits and deductions that apply to your specific situation.

Note that contribution levels and eligibility requirements change from year to year. For the most current information, check with the IRS at www.irs.gov.

## Roth IRA

You set up a Roth IRA with a bank, financial planner, or mutual fund company, just as you would a traditional IRA. But the Roth is quite different from the traditional IRA. First, you pay into a Roth with plain old after-tax dollars. No pre-tax contributions, no tax deductions. So why go Roth? Well, it might pinch a little at first, but it feels really good later when you withdraw your money—and pay no taxes.

It's an oversimplification to suggest that choosing between a traditional IRA and a Roth IRA is simply choosing between paying taxes now or later. Because you're not paying the same taxes. With a traditional IRA, you don't know what rate you'll be paying because you don't have a crystal ball to tell you what tax bracket you'll be in and what the tax code of year 2061 will look like. And, of course, you'll be taxed on the account earnings. With a Roth, you pay up front according to your current tax rate, then your money grows tax-free.

Things to know about the Roth IRA:

- **Expect fees.** Shop around. Inform yourself.

- **Early withdrawal.** You can withdraw your money early without penalties if you're 59 ½ and have held the account for at least 5 years.

- **No tax deduction.** Unlike traditional IRAs, Roth IRA contributions can not be deducted from your taxes.

- **Benefacting.** You are not required to take your money out of a Roth when you reach age 70 ½ , so you can leave the money, if you are inclined, tax-free to your heirs. Traditional IRAs do not allow this.

- **Contribution limits.** Like the traditional IRA, the maximum contribution limit is $5,500 (in 2014).

- **Eligibility rules.** If you're single and your adjusted gross income exceeds $129,000 or if you're married, filing jointly, and your income exceeds $191,000, you don't meet the eligibility rules for full contribution to a Roth IRA. (2011 figures.)

As with the traditional IRA, you can find the best information about Roth IRA eligibility by going straight to the source—the IRS website (www.irs.gov). For a clear and broad overview of these topics, check out the Pension Rights Center's website at www.pensionrights.org.

This is a lot of information to take in and it can be overwhelming. Even though we've included a lot of details here, the best thing you can do now is to stop reading, stop ruminating, planning, and weighing options. Just act. Start participating now. Maybe you don't have your dream job or your "real" job yet—no matter. Don't wait until everything lines up perfectly. Take what you can afford now, and put it into an interest-bearing account. If you work for an employer that does automatic contributions, definitely sign up, even if it's for a modest amount. At some point, you've got to take the single step to start the journey. If you take it now, you'll thank yourself later.

# THE GET OUT OF DEBT PLAN

## CHAPTER 7

Since we're dealing with the heart-stopping, palm-sweating topic of debt, let's start with a non-threatening, empowering exercise of association. Ready? OK, if your debt were an animal, what kind of animal would it be? And if your debt were a sound, what sound would it be? Last one: If your debt were a building, what kind of building would it be?

If you responded "gnat," "silence," and "gazebo," you do not need this chapter. Move on to the Saving for Retirement chapter or, better yet, the What It's Like to Be Completely Different From Other Members of My Generation chapter. (Seriously, congratulations.)

Now, if you answered that your debt "animal" would be a wolf, your debt "sound" would be a howl, and your debt "building" would be a jail, this chapter is for you.

Here's what you won't get if you read on: A quick fix or a magic bullet. But you also won't get a guilt trip. We assume you already know the basics about debt and are at the point where you need some simple encouragement to keep you focused on a debt-free or at least low-debt future. We also assume you're ready to face the debt you accrued during college and are looking forward to digging yourself out of the hole, whether that hole is a product of uncontrollable circumstances, spending habits, or a combination of both.

What you need now is a refresher on the types of debt you probably face, how to tackle that debt, and resources to help you along the way. So for now just ignore the strange animal sounds and concentrate not on the past, but what you can do in the present to shape your future.

## The good, the bad, and the ugly

We promised no guilt trips and we'll keep that promise, but we need to use some judgment words in order to outline the types of debt you likely face. Financial advisers and other money experts, including the loan officer who may someday decide if you're a good candidate for a low-interest home loan, generally see debt that works as an investment and has tax advantages as good. Student and home loans tend to be "good" debt.

It's important to remember that your student loan is an investment. Even if you owe $25,000 for a degree in one of those fields not generally known as lucrative, say philosophy, you will experience a payoff. It may be nonmaterial, but likely it will entail some material gain as well. Statistically, people with post-secondary degrees do much better in the job market than those who don't have them.

Because of the importance of a college education, student loans are generally viewed as low interest, high return investments. Much like home loans, they have the potential to offer higher future income. Also, both of these types of debts offer tax advantages—generally, you can write off a portion of the interest, which pulls down the cost of the debt itself.

That's the good. Now for the bad and the ugly. First, credit cards. Credit card debt is not necessarily bad or ugly in and of itself. In fact, some credit card use is necessary and "good" for building your FICO score. Also, using credit cards for some purchases gives you extra insurance. And credit cards tend to be much better than cash when, for instance, you travel and want to get the best exchange rate.

Credit card debt is bad debt, however, when it involves a double-digit interest rate and you're only able to make the minimum payment every month. Credit card debt is also bad when it's the product of living beyond one's means. Again, no guilt trip—the boots have been purchased and the weekend trip to Paduka is a distant memory—but if you're reading this chapter you're ready to avoid further frivolous charges on your credit card. So when to use the card? The car breaks down and you have no other way to pay for it? OK, put it on the card. Want the latest electronic tablet? Keep the plastic tucked away.

When is credit card debt downright ugly? The ugliness depends on how much you owe. How long will it take you to pay the debt down? How high is the interest rate? Is it limiting other opportunities, such as your ability to apply for a home loan? The answers to those questions will tell you when your credit card load has moved from bad to ugly.

## Get a handle on your debt

Like many money-related issues, it is easier to talk or read about debt than to actually face it. But you've made a commitment to keep reading and you're ready to look at the big picture. So, here's how to tackle debt:

**Step 1: Figure out what you owe.** Pull out your latest credit card and student loan statements and compile a list of the amount you owe to each vendor, interest rates, and minimum monthly payments. (Note: You can go to www. nslds.ed.gov, the National Student Loan Data System website, to see all of your student loans in one handy place).

**Step 2: Prioritize pay offs.** You need to make the minimum monthly payments on all debts or your credit score will suffer. But creditors' required minimum monthly payments are designed to pad their pockets and raid yours, so figure out how to pay more than the minimum. Pay off higher interest loans first. If Card A has an 18% rate, Card B has a 12% rate, and your student loans are at 7%, pay the minimum on the student loans and Card B, but pay Card A off as quickly as possible. If you type "debt calculator" into your search engine, you'll find some helpful and free calculating tools that will be useful for this step.

### Beware the Minimum Monthly Payment

**Consider Jill:** She owes $1,000 at 18% interest to Credit Card Z. If she pays the monthly minimum, it will take 153 months to pay that baby off—and she'll pay a total of $1,115 in interest. That's right, more than double her initial debt load.

If Jill pays a fixed amount of just $40 a month, which is more than twice the initial minimum monthly payment required, it will take 32 months to pay off the card and she'll pay $262 in interest. Still not ideal, but much better than the first scenario.

**Step 3: Consolidate debt.** We don't necessarily mean to consolidate your debt "officially," using a for-profit company to manage your accounts. After all, those places have to make their profit from somebody, and you would end up paying out more money—sometimes significantly more—than if you took care of it on your own. If you can pull all of your credit card debt onto one low-interest card, do it. It will lower your overall interest payments and allow you to pay one bill instead of several, thereby increasing your odds of paying the bill on time and keeping your credit score up.

### Pay Day Loans

Short-term loan vendors are notoriously good at squeezing every last drop out of their customers. Walk into one of those places, write them a check, and all of a sudden you have a little cash. **BUT**: The cost is sometimes as high as a 200%, even over 300%, APR. Check out the payday loan alert at www.ftc.gov for more information.

**Step 4: Stay focused.** Make it your mission to pay down debt and keep your charts, goals, and other notes in plain sight so you don't forget the big picture. Not only will you be in a better financial place later if you tackle debts now, you'll also experience mental and emotional relief when you take control of the issue.

### Free Credit Counseling

Do you feel over your head with debt? Even if you're treading the water and not drowning, it might be a good idea to talk with a counselor at the National Foundation for Credit Counseling (www.nfcc.org) or Consumer Credit Counseling Services (www.cccsstl.org). Both are no - to low-cost nonprofit organizations that offer education and counseling. It's worth checking out their websites!

So this chapter could be summarized as follows: Debt might look like a dragon and sound like a hyena, but it's really just a pile of numbers you need to face and, sometimes, rearrange. Avoid adding to your debt and definitely pay over the minimum required and you will pull yourself out of the hole. Student loans offer more flexibility and grace than other debts. Learn more about paying off student loans in Chapter 11. Explore all options, consult reliable nonprofit resources, and remember that the only bad decision is ignoring your debt.

**Consider This ...**

## Should I raid my savings to pay off debt?

The answer to this question varies depending on the situation. Savings accounts tend to earn about 1%, while credit cards often charge 12% or even more. Simple math says that you'll end up keeping more of your money if you pay off the high interest debt faster. Ask: Have I kicked the habits that racked up the credit card debt? If the answer is no, then you need to be cautious about draining your savings because you could find yourself in more debt and without a safety net down the line, especially if you're faced with an unforeseen emergency expense that requires you to rack up credit expenses you just paid off. And when it comes to paying off student loans with savings, most financial advisors say to hold off, though your individual situation might give you reason to consider that option. As for the retirement account...do everything you can to maintain it! (See Chapter 6, *Thought About Retirement?* for all the reasons not to withdraw retirement early.)

# SET GOALS AND MAKE TRADE-OFFS

## CHAPTER 8

What do you want to be when you grow up? For a five-year-old, the response is usually effortless: A firefighter. A superhero. A ballerina and an elephant. As we get older, we change our answers, but still fixate on that one question, as if it's the only one that matters.

While other people may persist in asking what you are or what you want to be, it's time to change the questions you ask yourself. Your profession is important—especially if you followed through on that early childhood plan and actually became a superhero—but *what* you are is less important than *who* you are. Questions that matter most to your life now are, *Who do I want to be?* and *What do I want to do?* In your search for the answers to these questions, you will need to reflect on your personal values. Part of this search entails understanding your relationship with money and figuring out how your life goals mesh with your financial goals.

It's time to spend a little time with your most trusted experienced life coach and financial advisor: a pad of paper. If you have that, a pencil, and a little bit of time, you can begin to design the life you want.

## Defining your goals

**TIP**
Setting clear goals gives you **vision** and **motivation.**

All goals should...
- be measurable
- have a timetable
- involve a strategy

Here's a start: Sit down and write a list of all the dreams and goals you have in mind. Be as specific as possible. Don't just write "travel" if what you really want is to "kayak the Amazon." Try to segment your goals into stages: think short term (today, this week, within the year), mid-range (1 – 5 years), and long- range (5 + years). Don't edit as you go—this list is for your eyes only and is subject to change. Be as specific as possible.

Once you've written up a comprehensive list, go through it and check all of the items related to money. Then begin a second list, this one with your money-related goals arranged in order of importance. As you prioritize, edit and refine.

You're much more likely to achieve a goal if it's specific and measurable and involves an action plan and timetable. It's not enough to say "I want to be independently wealthy." What does "wealthy" mean? (Having twenty thousand dollars in the bank? Owning a medium-sized city? Controlling Dubai from a manmade, charmingly dolphin-shaped island?) When do you want to achieve this? (In 40 years?

### Benefits of Goal Setting

**Good To Know**

Coaches, corporate advisors, and academics agree that people who set clear, measurable goals for themselves tend to be more focused, more self-confident, and more successful.

By next Thursday?) How will you accomplish it? (Redesigning the talking beer bottle opener? Selling bonds? Teaching English as a second language in Madison, Wisconsin?)

Make sure you include the occasional splurge in your short-term goals—you should enjoy your first paid vacation, for instance, and you may want a few new outfits to celebrate your first real job. If you treat yourself occasionally in this way, you will be more likely to reach those long-term goals.

Keep your goal worksheet in a handy place so you can check and revise it periodically.

### Example Financial Goals Worksheet

| Goal | Money Needed | Strategy | Timeline |
|------|-------------|----------|----------|
| 1. Pay off student loans | $16,000 | • Consolidate loans<br>• Make extra payment of $125/month | December 2016 |
| 2. Buy a "starter" home in the North End | $30,000 for down payment | • Build excellent credit score<br>• Telecommute two days a week; put transportation savings toward house<br>• Save $400 per month in dedicated account<br>• Once student loan is paid off, contribute same amount toward down payment account | June 2020 |

## Making trade-offs

Now that you've pinned your dreams to paper, you might feel overwhelmed. There are so many things to do, places to go, purchases you want to make, yet you're already incredibly busy and perhaps pressured by debt. Your salary's anemic, your "need" list long, your "want" list longer, the car's due for a tune-up, and it looks like you won't be able to afford a real vacation until 2041, when you finally drag that kayak to the Amazon.

Take a breath.

You can't do it all right now. Just do one thing. And no crash money diets—they work about as well as crash food diets (which is to say, they don't work at all). As with many things in life, you need to find a financial balance that will allow you to enjoy life in the present as you prepare for the future.

Make trade-offs along the way. You might decide, for example, to keep driving the junker for two years longer than originally planned in order to save more money for a down payment on a house. Or you might find that your original entertainment budget of $8 a month was too stringent, as it barely covered the price of your favorite martini.

Your goals for the future are meant to motivate and inspire you, not change you into a hermit. Build in some expenses for pleasure. If you switch from eating out every day to packing lunches, for example, you can go out for happy hour on Friday and still come out $25 ahead. Sure, if you cut back on all social dining you'd reach one of your long-term big goals a little sooner; you decide what the trade-off is worth.

## Take Action

To Do!

Feeling antsy? Want to stop sitting around writing out goals, dreaming up plans, and designing spreadsheets? Great! Here are some things you can do right now to fire up your action plan:

☐ **Check on your retirement account. Figure out what percentage it's earned the past quarter and year.**

☐ **Call your bank to ask if there are checking account options you're not using that will help you save some money. (For example, will you get free checking if your paycheck is deposited automatically?)**

☐ **Set up online payments for every merchant who accepts them.**

☐ **Cancel your landline if you really just use your cell phone.**

☐ **Turn off lights you aren't using.**

☐ **Place unwanted items up for sale on Craigslist or eBay.**

Revisit your long-term goals frequently to remind you that the way you get, spend, and keep your money is a personal choice. Some of the goals will be more challenging and you can expect unforeseen obstacles, but remember: You can do it. (Hey, you survived adolescence, right? What's better proof of resilience than that?)

## CHAPTER 9

# MAKING PERSONAL FINANCES PERSONAL

Time for some meta-visualization (sometimes we have to throw in those terms so our parents know all those years at college taught us something). Imagine yourself in the future—take it three years out, then ten years, then thirty. Are you active? Productive? Fulfilled? Energized? Engaged in meaningful work? (Yes, it sounds like an infomercial, but you are visualizing, after all, so might as well do it up. Give yourself white teeth, good knees, and a full head of hair while you're at it.) And what does your financial picture look like out there in the future? Are you solvent? Do you have a nest egg? Can you afford to travel/pay for the kids' braces/contribute to your favorite causes?

Good. Now let's talk about making that happen. The most significant first step is to realize that you are in control. Sure, you are tied to others in this world and beholden to some, but you have power no matter how broke you are or how much debt you have. You control your knowledge, actions, and attitude.

## Know what to know

Knowledge is power: It's cliché because it's true. What's in your account is less important than what's in your brain. A lot of people, however, don't really like to think about money beyond "If I had more, I could…." If you want to get to that place you visualized earlier, you've got to think about finances frequently and deliberately. This is not about being greedy or money-hungry, but about taking care of the inevitable business side of life so that it doesn't "take care" of you.

Here's how to get control of your finances through knowledge:

1. Understand your relationship with money (see top of next page).

2. Know what's coming in and what's going out.

3. Understand how your remaining income is working for you.

4. Inform yourself using reputable sources: Ask questions; read articles, books, and websites; go to the occasional seminar or workshop.

5. Do Steps 1 – 4 in no particular order, over and over and over again.

It sounds like a full-time job, but it doesn't have to be. Don't worry about reading every prospectus and every article you come across. Do what you can when you can and you'll learn as you go. It's worth making your financial self-education a priority. You work hard; it'd feel great to make the most of your earnings.

## Know the best sources

Finding information is not a problem. Plug the phrase "best mutual funds" into your search engine and you'll get about 16,000,000 hits. Even if researching mutual funds *is* your full time job, you need to know how to identify the truly useful information or you'll drown in the mire of the Web, where little Kaylee Drebber's 5th grade research project and gimmicky self-professed money gurus pop up right next to Forbes, Money Magazine, and the Better Business Bureau.

Separate the useful from the useless (and determine affiliation and bias) by following these tips:

**Ask people you know and trust.** What sources do they rely on for financial information?

**Read the articles that apply to you.** If you have time to learn about onion futures, go for it. But if you're schedule is tight, focus on the material that will benefit you immediately.

**Check authorship.** Who wrote the piece? Who published it? Many for-profit websites contain helpful information, but if you're learning about the art of CD laddering from a bank website, expect an underlying sales pitch.

**Notice advertising.** If that financial guru on TV gets advertising dollars from James K. Polk Investments, his advice might tilt toward the advertiser even if it's not the best choice for his audience.

**Find "go-to" sources.** These should be books or websites that have proven to be helpful, thorough, and accurate. That way, when you're doing some rushed researching, you'll get solid answers fast.

**Check three.** Before you make any financial decision, check with at least three trusted sources. Even if you have a financial adviser, you need to ensure *you're* well informed and have the tools to make sound decisions.

**Go slow.** If it's a hot deal and you've got to act fast or you'll lose out…pass. Any decision you make will involve a degree of uncertainty, but pinning all hopes on the sounds-too-good-to-be-true opportunity is like believing that, if you're really, really nice this year, Santa will swoop down and pay off your student loans.

## Financial personal trainers and certified financial advisers

There are benefits to working with a financial advisor: They save you time, might get higher returns than you would on your own, and provide an objective view that can help keep you focused on your financial goals.

It might feel strange to entrust your finances to a third party. It *should* feel strange—there's significant risk involved. Arm yourself with some basic knowledge and you'll be in good shape.

### How do Financial Planners Earn a Living?

*GooD To KNow*

Here are the most common ways financial planners make money.

**Commissions.** Commission-based planners get money from brokerages every time they sell a product to you. Analogy: You go to a Honda dealership, they're going to try to sell you a Honda, even if the best car for you is actually a Volkswagon.

**Fees.** Fee-based planners charge a percentage of the assets they are helping you manage. The bigger the assets, the more they make. Some of these planners won't take on clients who don't meet a minimum asset threshold.

**Combination of Fees and Commissions.** Some planners charge to develop a plan, then collect commissions by selling you the things the plan comprises.

**Hourly/Flat Rates.** These planners charge you for their time, either by the hour or with a flat rate. They meet with you and help you develop a plan. You can follow through on the plan on your own or pay them more to do the legwork for you. These tend to be the least biased, but the situation does require more time on your part as well as more up-front money.

A good financial coach…

- Has strong references.
- Helps, advises, sympathizes, and praises.
- Asks first: What are your goals? What financial problems do you have? What assets and liabilities do you have?
- Develops a workable strategy and reviews it regularly with you.
- Contacts you regularly.

Beware of the financial adviser who…

- Asks first: How much money do you have to invest?

- Asks you to make out checks to him or her personally. Except for fees, all checks for investments should be in the name of the brokerage or mutual fund.

- Lists him or herself as a joint owner or beneficiary on any of your accounts.

- Signs your name to documents.

- Does not contact you regularly.

You can also seek help from a friend, relative, coworker—someone you trust and who has experience and sound financial judgment. Do protect yourself—and your relationship with this trusted person—by always following up any advice with your own research. That way you'll gain confidence in your own judgment. Plus, you'll be able to give yourself some credit for the good decisions and won't be tempted to blame your "trainer" if an investment bonks.

If you do decide to work with a paid professional, start your research by asking friends and family for their recommendations.

**TIP** **Interviewing a Prospective Financial Planner**

When you interview a financial advisor, take your time and don't be shy about asking questions. It's a big commitment and you will feel more confident if you're thorough at this stage of the process. Following are important questions to ask:

- How do you charge for your services?
- Do you perform other services, like tax or legal advising?
- What qualifies you to be my financial coach?
- How long have you been a financial planner?
- How many clients do you have? How big is the asset base you manage for those clients?
- What kind of liability insurance do you carry?
- Do you currently work with clients in a comparable financial situation to mine?
- Do you have references available?
- Once the plan is complete, how will I implement it?

## Action and attitude

All of the advice-seeking and research should go a long way toward making you feel like an informed, capable investor and consumer. If you tend to act rashly, you might have to train yourself to take the time to investigate your options. If, on the other hand, you're the type who could research, take notes, cross-reference, and analyze for months before making a decision, remember the risks of inaction, such as lapsed health insurance, or loss of earnings. (Same advice goes for relationships, but that's for another book.)

Getting to that glorious, financially solvent future requires research, action, and a confident attitude. Confidence here means you can look squarely at your current financial situation and make a plan for your future one. It's really not so much about *taking* control as it is about *recognizing*—and acting upon—the control you already have.

# CREDIT CARDS

## CHAPTER 10

Ah, credit cards! So small, so shiny, so easy to use. So necessary when "cash flow problem" is just a euphemism for "downright broke." Credit cards are convenient and secure. You're not likely to rush to the airport to pay for a flight with a wad of cash; you're even less likely to call the bank to put a stop payment on the cash someone lifted from your wallet. Credit cards allow you to book flights and hotels, they provide extra insurance for some purchases, and they tend to be much better than cash when you travel and want to get the best exchange rate. Credit cards—and their numbers—can and do get stolen, but the consumer is usually protected when that happens. This means you probably won't be responsible for charges racked up illegally with your card.

There's a flip side, of course. Because they are so easy to use, they're also easy to misuse. Their convenience can lead to impulse shopping. More than a few of us have racked up more debt than we intended to and are surprised by our credit card balances. On top of that, interest rates that begin as low, introductory rates quickly become unmanageably high. Furthermore, when you make only the minimum monthly payment, either out of choice or necessity, you end up paying doubly or even triply for that purchase you made five years ago.

Despite the potential risks of misusing credit cards, they are helpful for building and maintaining one's overall credit, which can affect everything from future employment to the ability to buy a home.

This chapter will provide an overview of the types of credit cards available, terms related to credit cards and interest, and how to monitor credit cards.

## Choosing a credit card

Chances are you already have a credit card or two or three. The average under-graduate student, after all, has 4.6 credit cards, according to a 2009 Sallie Mae study. However, as you begin your post-college life, you may be in the market for a credit card that better fits your current needs. Here are some of the major types of credit cards available:

**Standard:** Standard, or traditional, credit cards include balance transfer and low-interest cards. They generally offer convenience, security, but few perks.

**Premium:** Premium cards are available to people with excellent credit who want some perks, which might include travel or gas points, savings on events or at hotels, cash back, etc.

**Affinity:** Affinity cards enable you to show your connection to your favorite charity or organization, including your alumni association. With each swipe of your affinity card, up to .3% of the transaction is donated to your cause.

**Airline:** Many airlines offer their own line of credit cards. Consumers use these cards to earn mileage as they spend money. If you are inclined to go for a mileage card, you might want to wait for one of the frequent promotional periods to sign up, when you can get a bunch of miles all at once.

**Retail:** You know the drill: You're checking out with your basket full of stuff, and the clerk says robotically, "And do you have a Target (or Gap or Sears or World Market) credit card? You could save 10% on your purchases today if you get one." These cards usually don't entail an application or annual fee, but their interest rates tend to be pretty high. Also, keep in mind that retail cards rarely benefit your credit score, but they can damage it if you don't manage them.

**Secured and prepaid:** These credit cards are usually used by people who are trying to rebuild their credit. With a secured credit card, you pay an up-front security deposit for the ability to access credit. The more you deposit, the more credit will be available to you. With a prepaid card, you basically "fill it up" and use it until it's drained.

Of course, there are lots of other factors to consider when choosing a credit card. People with poor credit will have fewer options available to them than those who have good credit. When you compare the various cards available to you, you'll want to think about the interest rate, annual and other fees you'll have to pay, perks available with each card, and whether or not those perks are worth any extra expense the card entails.

## Interest rates

Interest is the price you pay for using credit. When you shop around for a credit card, you'll want to find one that charges you the least interest. If you have excellent credit you are more likely to be eligible for low-interest credit cards; people with poor credit often end up paying much higher interest.

To entice consumers, many companies will offer low- or no-interest introductory periods on certain transaction types. Ideally, we would all pay off our credit card balances each month and therefore not have to worry so much about the interest rate. However, the reality is that most of us carry a balance from month to month. In 2013, according to CreditCards.com, the average unpaid credit card balance was over $4,800. And the average interest rate was about 13.11%. (By the way, Joe Average with a $4,800 credit card balance and 13.11% interest will take 20 years to pay off that balance—and pay a total of $5,030 in interest if he pays only the minimum balance.)

If you do pay off your credit card balance each month, you won't be charged interest at all. Savvy consumers use their credit cards regularly but pay no interest and little to no fees. They enjoy the security of purchasing with a credit card, along with some added perks, such as racking up airline mileage or rebate points.

For the rest of us—who might be savvy but still carrying a credit card balance from month to month—the interest rate is very important. Following are definitions and explanations of some key terms related to credit card interest rates:

**Annual percentage rate (APR):** This is the yearly interest rate the credit card company charges you. There are **fixed-rate APRs** and **variable APRs**. **Fixed-rate APRs** are set at one interest rate. That interest rate can change—but by law the credit card company would have to notify you of the change in terms 45 days before the change takes place. You would then have time to "opt out" and close your account with that company. (Of course, you would be obligated to repay the remaining balance.)

**Variable APRs** are tied to an index, such as the prime rate. If your credit card agreement states that the APR is "prime + 8%", you could be charged 10.99% in one billing cycle when the prime rate is 3% and 15.99% in another billing cycle, if the prime rate moves up to 8%. This is an extreme example, but it is true that variable APRs can fluctuate widely. Most credit cards have a variable APR.

When you read the terms and conditions of your credit card offer, you will probably see several APRs listed. Why? Well, there are a few types of transactions you can make with a credit card. You can purchase something, of course. You can also transfer your balances from one card to another. And you can get a cash advance. Each of these types of transactions might be subject to a different APR. And if you make a late payment, your APR(s) will almost certainly increase.

Let's say you apply for a low-interest credit card that offers a 0% APR for the first year. That 0% APR might apply only to new purchases; balance transfers and cash advances might have altogether different rates. Take a look at this terms disclosure from a hypothetical lender we'll call the Bank of Plastic (we've added the notes and sound effects):

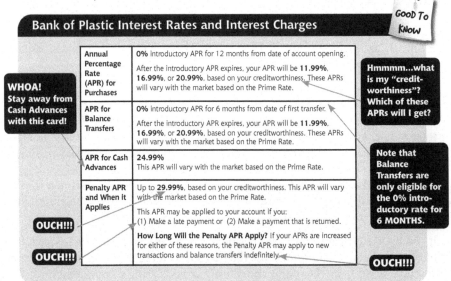

As you can see in this example, there are 6 APRs specified in the disclosure. Which ones apply to you will depend on the types of transactions you make, your "creditworthiness," and whether or not you make a late payment.

## Credit card fees

The "go-to" rate is the interest rate you are charged after the introductory rate expires. **TIP**

There seem to be as many fees as there are credit card designs, though of course the fees are not as shiny or good looking. Here are some of the more common fees you'll encounter when you're shopping for a credit card or reading over your credit card statement:

**Application fee:** Some companies charge a fee for applying for a card with them. This is also sometimes called a **processing fee.**

**Annual fee:** Many cards have a yearly fee for using their card. This is also sometimes called a membership fee.

**Inactivity fee:** This is the current "It" fee, the popular one all the banks seem to be adding in the wake of the 2009 Credit CARD Act that limited other types of fees. Cancel any credit cards you aren't using or you might very well end up paying…to not use them.

**Penalty fees:** If you make a late payment, you'll get nabbed with a late **payment fee**. If you go over your credit limit, you're likely to incur an **over-the-limit fee**. A returned payment will result in a—you guessed it!— **returned payment fee**. Any kind of penalty will also likely result in an increase in the interest you pay. Ouch, ouch, and ouch!

In 2009, Americans spent an estimated $20 billion on credit card penalty fees. **GOOD TO KNOW**

Source: www.creditcards.com

**Balance transfer fee:** When you transfer your debt from one card to another, you pay. It may be a fixed amount or a percentage of the amount transferred (usually, the greater of the two.) Even if the up-front fee to transfer is high, it might be worth it if you're transferring a balance from a very high interest card to a very low interest card—and you plan on paying it off.

**Cash advance fee**: Like the balance transfer fee, the cash advance fee may be a fixed amount or a percentage of the transaction.

The Federal Reserve Board's website (www.federalreserve.gov) and CreditCards.com have more information about standard (and some not-so-standard) credit card fees.

## Monitoring your credit cards

In any relationship, it's important to touch base once in a while to reassess how things are going. OK, so you won't sit down with your credit card and discuss feelings, but you should reevaluate them every once in a while. Here are some tips for monitoring your credit cards:

**Check your interest rate.** Most people do not know their current interest rates. If they checked, they might find that it's time to transfer to a card with a lower interest rate.

**Check your activity.** Because more banks are starting to charge inactivity fees, you should know which cards you're holding are costing you money. You might want to cancel some. However: Remember that you'll have higher credit scores if you have a lot of credit available to you but you aren't using a very high percentage of it. In other words, it might be worth it to keep a lame credit card in your file just to keep your credit score looking good.

**Read your statements.** New legislation mandates that credit card companies convey information about fees, APRs, and the true cost of paying just the minimum balance in each statement. However, if you don't read that statement, you won't know any of this information.

**Know your numbers.** Know how many credit cards you have, their numbers, and the names and contact information of the companies that issued them. You might need this information if you fall victim to identity theft.

**Protect your credit cards.** Use them only on secured sites, give out the numbers only to people you have good reason to trust. (See Chapter 12 on Identity Theft for more information.)

### Always pay more than the minimum!

**TIP**

- If you have a $2,000 balance on a credit card that charges 19% interest, it will take you over 8 years and almost another $2,000 to pay it off if you just make the minimum monthly payments.
- Use the Federal Reserve Board's credit card calculator www.federalreserve.gov/creditcardcalculator/ to determine how long it will take you to pay off your balances.

Whether you're just starting out and will soon be getting your first credit card or you've already got the average 4.6 cards, remember to always pay more than the minimum amount due and always, always pay on time. Doing so will help you build excellent credit—or, if need be, repair credit that's already damaged.

# STUDENT LOANS

## CHAPTER 11

If you're like many well-educated people in your generation, you not only have a degree, you also have, according to the Project on Student Debt, over $25,000 in student loan debt. More if you took on graduate school. Even more if you went to medical school. Because of the ever-increasing costs of tuition and housing (and textbooks!), a majority of graduates leave school with a diploma and a hefty load of student loans. For many the debt they carry is absolutely staggering.

So what do you do with those loans now that you're out of school and actually expected to pay them back? One idea is to wrap a large monument—say, the Statue of Liberty—with loan statements and lecture notes, then make a documentary about the experience. You'll become a famous artist and your worries will center on "the nature of postmodern experience" rather than the mundane "trying to pay all my bills on a starter salary." But the best approach to your student loans is probably to pay them back.

Luckily, federal student loans are a pretty forgiving species: If you experience financial hardship you can make a quick phone call, fill out a form, and— voila!—you just might qualify for a deferment or forbearance. On the other hand, if you default on a student loan you'll look really, really flaky, experience a drop in your credit score, and might even have your wages garnished, a friendly word that means "hand over your paycheck."

## Know your loans and lenders

Many people have multiple student loans. The first step to dealing with your student loans is figuring out what you owe and to whom. Whether you have a Perkins, a Stafford (also known as Federal Direct), or a PLUS loan, all of your federal student loan information is in one convenient spot: the National Student Loan Data System (www.nslds.ed.gov). If you have private loans they will not be included in the NSLDS.

Make sure to notify your loan servicers when you move or change your contact information! You are responsible for making complete and timely student loan payments, even if you haven't received a bill or notice.

### Should I Pay Off Student Loans Early?

*Consider This ...*

Yes! If you can, and other "bad" debt is paid off, and you've invested in retirement, by all means pay down that student loan. Important tip: Make sure you note on the payment that your intention is to pay down the principal, not just to make an early payment.

## Student Loan Vocabulary

**Capitalized:** When unpaid interest is added to the principal of the loan. Example: Paul has a $10,000 student loan in forbearance. If Paul pays nothing toward that student loan for 12 months, and the interest rate is 6%, he will owe $10,616.78 at the end of the year instead of the original $10,000.

**Deferment:** Postponement of payments on a loan. If you have a subsidized loan, interest will not accrue during deferment.

**Disbursement:** Payment of funds from the lender

**Discharged:** Cancelled.

**Forbearance:** A temporary postponement or reduction of payments on a loan. During forbearance, interest will accrue.

**Principal:** The amount of money borrowed.

## Repayment

As the government student financial aid websites remind us, student loans are something we are obligated to pay back no matter how we feel about our educational experience or what kind of job we end up with. That's not a shock to most of us, but actually making monthly payments on those loans for 5, 10, even 25 years can be shocking. The first student loan bill seems to arrive along with the diploma—and well before the paychecks start rolling in.

In fact, if you have a Direct PLUS Loan, the repayment period begins immediately after the final loan disbursement and your first payment is due within 60 days, which may well be before your graduation.

However, if you have a Federal Perkins loan or a Federal Direct Stafford Loan, you are allowed a grace period before you need to start paying off your loans. The day after you graduate your grace period begins. From that date, you'll have 6 months if you have a Federal Direct Stafford Loan and 6 - 9 months if you have a Federal Perkins Loan before you enter what's called the repayment period. This repayment period is, of course, when you're expected to make regular, complete, monthly payments.

> **The longer the term of your loan, the more you'll pay.** _TIP_

There are several student loan repayment plans available. You might choose one repayment plan at first and then switch if your circumstances change. Here are the options:

**Standard Repayment Plan:** Under this plan, you will have fixed monthly payments for up to 10 years. Your monthly payment will be at least $50 ($40 for a Perkins Loan). You'll pay less interest with this plan than with the others because you'll pay off your loan more quickly, but higher monthly payments might be difficult to manage as a new graduate. Note: This is the "default" repayment plan. In other words, unless you specifically request another repayment plan you will be assigned this one.

**Graduated Repayment Plan:** This plan also allows up to 10 years for repayment. However, the payments are lower at first and increase every two years. The idea is to pay less when you're just starting out and more as your income grows.

**Extended Repayment Plan:** With this plan, you get up to 25 years to repay your student loan—as long as you have over $30,000 in Direct Loan debt. You may choose fixed or graduated monthly payments. The benefit to choosing the Extended Repayment Plan is that you will have smaller, more manageable monthly payments than you would with the Standard Repayment Plan. The

## Consider the hypothetical case of a student we'll call Collin. *Consider This...*

If Collin has a $35,000 Federal Direct Unsubsidized Loan (also called a Federal Stafford Unsubsidized Loan) with an interest rate of 6.8%, his monthly payment could be as **low as $198** and as **high as $403**, depending on which of the above three plans he chooses. And that original $35,000 loan will ultimately cost him between $48,333 and $78,939. Go to http://studentaid.ed.gov/ to calculate your loan payments.

| Standard Repayment Plan | Extended Repayment Plan |
|:---:|:---:|
| **$403 / month** | **$198 / month** |
| TOTAL = $48,333 | TOTAL = $78,939 |

downside is that you pay more interest when you take more time to pay off a loan.

There are two other repayment plans, both of which offer even more flexibility than the first three—and a little more fine print:

**Income-Contingent Repayment (ICR) Plan:** With this plan, your required monthly payment is recalculated each year based on your income (and your spouse's income, if applicable), family size, and amount of your Direct Loan debt. If you cannot pay off the loan after 25 years, the unpaid amount will be forgiven, though you may have to pay taxes on that amount.

**Income-Based Repayment (IBR) Plan:** With the IBR Plan, your required monthly payment is based on your income and family size. You qualify for an IBR if you have a "partial hardship," which basically means that the monthly payments you would make on the 10-year standard repayment plan are higher than those you would be expected to make on the IBR Plan. (Use the calculator at www.studentaid.gov/ibr to see if you qualify.) Like the ICR Plan, your monthly payment may be adjusted every year. Both the IBR and the ICR Plans usually cost more in the long run than the Standard Repayment Plan, because it takes longer to pay down the loan and therefore the borrower pays more interest. However, you'll have lower monthly payments than a Standard Repayment Plan and the unpaid balance of your loan may be forgiven after 25 years if you meet certain conditions. One benefit to going with the IBR Plan is that if you have a Subsidized Stafford loan, the Federal Government will pay your accrued interest

**NOTE:** Because of the Health Care and Education Reconciliation Act of 2010, student loans taken out after July 1, 2014 will be even more forgiving. Borrowers will be expected to pay a smaller percentage of their discretionary income each month toward student loans and those loans will be forgiven after 20 years, instead of 25.

for up to three consecutive years from the time you sign on. One drawback is that you need to submit documentation every year that you're on the IBR Plan.

So, while you don't have a choice to repay your student loan, you do have plenty of choices of *how* to repay. We've provided an overview of your options here based on the most current information available through the U.S. Department of Education; however, each graduate's situation is unique and it's important to read through more detailed information about the different repayment plans to see which one will best fit your needs. The websites www.direct.ed.gov and http://studentaid.ed.gov, as well as the exit counseling you'll receive by law, are essential resources for all of your student loan questions.

## Defaulting

Defaulting on a loan means failing to meet the obligations of the contract. We mentioned in the introduction of this chapter that people who default risk a drop in their credit scores and having their wages garnished. (For more information about why you want to maintain a good credit score, see Chapter 1.) Additional possible consequences of defaulting include racking up fines in addition to your original debt and even being sued. Because defaulting is so serious, we strongly recommend signing up for automatic withdrawals to ensure you make your student loan payments on time. If you cannot keep up with your payments, contact the organization that services your loan and make arrangements right away.

## Options if you are unable to keep up with your payments

If you feel swamped with student loan debt and are unable to keep up with the payments no matter how much you cut living expenses, you have options for getting out of the mire:

**Deferment:** A deferment is a temporary "get out of monthly payments" pass. People interested in pursuing this option need to apply and qualify for it. (Another good reason not to default: You will not be eligible for a deferment if you do.) If you have a subsidized student loan and qualify for a deferment, interest will not accrue while you're deferring the loan. If you have an unsubsidized loan, interest will accrue and be capitalized (added to the principal balance), but your responsibility for payments will be postponed until later. To qualify for a deferment, you need to prove you are

- still in school (at least half-time), or
- unemployed, or
- suffering from economic hardship, or
- active duty military

Make certain you keep up with your payments while you are waiting for confirmation of your deferment or you might end up in default.

Note: Peace Corps and AmeriCorps volunteers may be eligible to defer their loans while in service and almost certainly qualify for forbearance (see below).

## Forbearance

Let's say you are not eligible for a deferment but still feel strapped by your student loan responsibilities. If this is the case, consider requesting a forbearance, which will allow you to postpone or reduce your monthly payments for a period of time (up to 12 months), while you get your footing. There are fewer obstacles to obtaining forbearance than a deferment. You need to demonstrate you are

- in poor health, or
- in a rigorous residency, or
- serving in AmeriCorps, Teach for America, or Peace Corps
- paying 20% or more of your monthly income to student loan debt

Unlike deferred subsidized loans, interest accrues and is capitalized (added to the principal balance) during the period of forbearance. Also, it's common to stretch out the length of the loan to reduce monthly minimums, which benefits the borrower in the short term but costs more in the long term.

Remember to keep up with your monthly payments while you are waiting for forbearance approval or you might end up in default.

> *Consider This...*
>
> ### Should You Consolidate?
>
> Plug in your own numbers using an online calculator:
> http://loanconsolidation.ed.gov/loancalc

## Consolidating student loans

When your student loan debt seems overwhelming, either because of the amounts involved or the number of bills you have to track each month, you might want to consider consolidating it. This is a popular method for dealing with student loans, though it isn't right for everybody.

> *Good To Know*
>
> ### The Perks of a Perkins
>
> If you have a Perkins or special, more difficult to qualify for loan, remember you'll lose benefits if you consolidate it. That nice, long grace period? Gone when consolidated. The lower interest rate? Averaged. And adios to any cancellation benefits. (Example: Some states offer loan forgiveness if you teach in a high-need area for a year or two. But consolidated loans are not eligible for these deals.)

Loan consolidation is the process of combining all current eligible loans into one. You end up with a fixed average interest rate and one monthly payment, which is generally lower than your current combined payments. To calculate interest, the lender uses a weighted average of your current loans and rounds it up to the nearest one-eighth of one percent. The interest rate for consolidated loans is currently capped at 8.25%. You have the same menu of repayment options available to you if you consolidate (Standard Repayment Plan, Extended Repayment Plan, Graduated Repayment Plan, etc.).

But there is a catch: The weighted average might not change your payments drastically. Also, the life of the loan will be increased in order to get to a low monthly payment. In short, you pay less monthly, but more in the long term. Also, you want to be careful which loans you consolidate, because some—like the Perkins, for example—have great benefits that you'll lose if you lump them with the others.

Let's take a look at how this would work with hypothetical graduate Karen. Karen's current student loan debt looks like this:

| Loan Amount | Type of Loan | Interest Rate | Number of Payments | Monthly Payment (Standard Plan) | Total Cost of Loan |
|---|---|---|---|---|---|
| $10,000 | Unsubsidized Stafford | 5.25% | 120 | $107 | $12,875 |
| $10,000 | Unsubsidized Stafford | 6.8% | 120 | $115 | $13,809 |
| $15,000 | Subsidized Stafford | 4.0% | 120 | $152 | $18,224 |

Her total monthly payment is $374 and the total she'll pay over the life of her loans, assuming she doesn't prepay them, is $44,908.

If Karen decides to consolidate, she would have a combined loan amount of $35,000. The weighted average calculates out to 5.25% and the amount she pays monthly as well as over the life of the loan depends on which repayment plan she chooses:

| Total Loan Amount: $35,000 Interest Rate: 5.25% | | | |
|---|---|---|---|
| Repayment Plan | Number of Payments | Initial Monthly Payment | Total Cost of Loan |
| Standard | 240 | $236 | $56,603 |
| Graduated | 240 | $153 | $61,990 |
| Extended (fixed) | 300 | $210 | $62,921 |
| Extended (graduated) | 300 | $153 | $68,858 |

So if Karen goes for the lowest possible monthly payment now by consolidating and selects the extended graduated repayment plan, it will mean nearly $24,000 more that she'll have to pay over the life of the loan.

There are a lot of factors missing from this scenario. For instance, Karen might have reason to believe that her income is going to increase exponentially in a year or two, which will allow her to pay off all of her debt. Without a crystal ball you won't know your best option until decades have passed, but you have all the resources you need to make the decision that you think is best for you now.

## Loan cancellation and forgiveness

Wouldn't it be nice to just call up your loan servicer and say, "I'd like the balance of my student loan cancelled, please!"? It's not that easy, but it is possible to have your federal student loans discharged (cancelled) or forgiven. Death, total disability, and bankruptcy are some of the more, ahem, extreme conditions which can erase your loans. Here are some other, more positive ways to get the same result:

**Public Service Loan Forgiveness Program (PSLF):** If you work full time in public service (for example, if you work for an emergency management organization or in public health or education), have not defaulted on your student loans, and have made 120 monthly payments toward your loans, you may qualify for the PSLF. See the PSLF factsheet at http://studentaid.ed.gov for more information.

**Stafford Loan Forgiveness Program for Teachers:** Teachers employed in high-needs areas may qualify for loan forgiveness after a certain number of years of service. Find out more about cancellation and deferment options for teachers at http://studentaid.ed.gov.

Consider This ...

## Things to Keep in Mind if You Decide to Consolidate:

- You can only consolidate your student loans once (unless you go back to school and take on additional student loan debt).
- You don't have to consolidate all of your student loans into one.
- Loan consolidation is free. If you are asked to pay a fee, you are working with the wrong company.
- You might receive a lower interest rate by:
  - ✔ Consolidating during your student loan grace period (generally the first six months after you graduate or go less than full time).
  - ✔ Signing up for automatic debit payments.
  - ✔ Making on time payments for 36 months straight.

You might also have the balance of your loans discharged if you make payments faithfully for at least 25 years through one of the extended repayment plans.

## A word about private student loans

This chapter focuses on federal student loans because they are the most common source of loans for U.S. students. However, you might have taken out a private student loan, so we'll include some tips for dealing with them now that you've graduated.

The first general guideline is that there is no general guideline: The conditions and terms of private student loans vary widely, since they are not tied to the same rules and regulations as the government's direct loan programs. For example, one bank might offer a loan at a 3% interest rate with minimal fees, while another bank might offer a loan at a 12% interest rate with substantial fees. More likely, a bank offers a loan at a variable interest rate, which means that your monthly payment could change drastically under a variety of circumstances.

Also, unlike the federal loans, which offer fairly accessible deferments, forbearance, and even cancellation, private lenders tend to be much less flexible. For example, someone who experiences a major medical issue or extreme financial hardship may have to continue his or her monthly payments to the private lender—or risk severe penalties. Each loan and lender is different, so make sure you know your rights and responsibilities related to any private student loans you hold.

No matter how burdensome your student loan seems some months, remember that it was—and is—an investment. Your federal student loans offer more flexibility and grace than other debts; you just might have to reevaluate your repayment program every few years to make sure you're on the plan that makes the most sense for your current financial situation as well as your financial future.

## Essential Student Loan Resources

**Everything you need to know about federal student loans:** www.direct.ed.gov and http://studentaid.ed.gov

**See what you owe and to whom:** National Student Loan Data System (www.nslds.ed.gov).

**Learn all about loan consolidation** at the U.S. Department of Education's website: www.loanconsolidation.ed.gov (or call 1-800-557-7392)

**Student Loan Borrower Assistance**, a comprehensive resource for student borrowers and their families: http://www.studentloanborrowerassistance.org/

# IDENTITY THEFT

## CHAPTER 12

Who are you? You might delve into the depths of this question in a philosophical discussion, but in this chapter we're mostly just talking about your name, your social security number, and your money.

Identity theft is when someone steals your name and personal information, such as your social security number, for their financial gain. According to the Federal Trade Commission, every year an estimated 9 million Americans have their identities stolen.

The cost of identity theft per victim varies because it can come in many forms. For example, if someone tries to purchase something with your credit card, but you find out about the breach right away and deal with it immediately, the financial cost to you will probably be zero. However, if someone opens a new credit card account using your social security number and you are unaware of the problem for several months, you might end up having to pay thousands of dollars out of pocket—and spending countless hours documenting the fraud and trying to repair the damage done to your credit score. Indeed, it can take years to take back your identity, which is not only a hassle but an emotional (and financial) strain as well.

## How identity thieves operate

We can probably assume we know *why* identity thieves do what they do: money, of course. *How* they do what they do is a different story. An identity thief could be a person who lives down the block who rummages through the recycling bins to find non-shredded credit card offers, or he or she could be someone you'll never meet who operates a sophisticated phishing scam out of another country. According to the Federal Trade Commission, here are some of the common ways the bad guys get your personal information:

**Stealing:** Sure, purses and wallets are valuable commodities, but identity thieves can also steal checks—and other mail that contains confidential information— out of your mailbox or your personal files from your employer's office. They can then use that information to open credit card accounts in your name.

**Dumpster diving:** Dumpster "digging" is the more appropriate term to use, as thieves dig through garbage and recycling bins to find credit card offers, bank statements, and other pieces of mail that can provide them with the information they want.

**Skimming:** Skimmers are small electronic devices that read the magnetic strip of your credit or debit card. They can be fitted onto an ATM machine or point of sale terminal, or simply carried by people who have access to your cards and want to scam you. Skimmers are not obvious to the untrained eye, so customers at ATM machines and pay-at-the-pump gas stations have inserted their debit cards into these scamming scanners and unknowingly compromised their bank accounts. There have also been cases of store clerks, waiters, and other people who have access to credit and debit cards surreptitiously swiping customers' cards. The card information is then immediately up for grabs, as the information is transferred electronically to anyone willing to pay a little for access to strangers' credit lines.

**Phishing:** Phishing is a cute name for a nasty type of fraud that involves bad guys "fishing" for people's personal information. According to the Federal Deposit Insurance Corporation (FDIC), here's how phishing works: You get an email that looks like it's from a reputable institution, such as your bank. The message requests that you "verify," "re-submit," or "confirm" some personal information. If you click on a link in the message, it will take you to a website that looks like the reputable institution's, but is actually fake. Any information you submit to this website will be available to the identity thieves.

**Pretexting:** Pretexting is when the thief gains access to your information under the pretext of doing something else. For example, a thief might call pretending to be from an organization you trust and convince you that he or she needs to verify some of your personal information. If you share that information, he or she can then use it to access your bank account.

**Keylogging:** Undetectable software that tracks keystrokes and websites visited. A malicious user (as opposed to the benign one who just wants to know what you're doing online all the time?) can glean your login names, passwords, and other information as you go about your daily business. Some keylogging software even provides screenshots to whoever it is who is monitoring.

## Why young adults are targets

We realize that not every recent graduate is a young adult, but many are in their early to mid-twenties—and therefore prime targets for identity fraud. In fact, according to a March 2010 *Washington Post* article, 18- to 24-year-olds are the most vulnerable when it comes to identify theft. Why? Because they receive frequent credit card applications, tend to store personal information on their computers and cell phones, and infrequently reconcile their bank or credit card balances. A quick response time is critical when it comes to limiting the damage caused by identity fraud; people who don't monitor their bills or reconcile their accounts regularly give thieves that much more time to do damage. Another reason the 18- to 24-year-old group is at risk for identity fraud is because they are so comfortable sharing personal information—whether it's using a credit card to buy something online, entering one's social security number in order to qualify for a promotional event, or posting one's age and date of birth on Facebook.

It's tempting to think that because you might not have many assets right now (a microwave, ten pairs of socks, and a copy of this book), there's nothing to steal. As Janis Joplin famously sang, "Freedom's just another word for nothing left to lose." However, you do have something to lose: thieves can steal your future earnings—and your peace of mind—by racking up debt in your name and trashing your credit score.

## Preventing identity theft

One reason so many young adults think nothing of sharing their personal information may be because it seems like identity theft is unavoidable, an annoying price to pay for access and convenience. However, there are effective steps you can take to help prevent identity theft:

- Shred credit card applications and other documents that might contain personal information

- Keep copies of all active credit cards and bank account numbers under lock and key—they should be available so you can cancel them at a moment's notice, but protected

- Use a firewall on your computer

- Carefully and immediately review bank documents and financial aid documents

- Keep your PINs and passwords to yourself

- Use strong PINs and passwords

- Check your credit report on a regular basis

- Guard your social security number, date of birth, and other personal information

- Verify the source before you provide information to someone claiming to be with a legitimate organization

**Too many passwords? Not enough?** | *To Do!*

How many passwords do you have to keep track of? A dozen? More? Or do you just use the same one or two for every account? Ideally, of course, you'd have a unique, intricate password for every account and password-protected website. The easiest, most secure, way to achieve that ideal is to create those passwords, write them down on paper, and tuck them away where you can find them but others can't. Another way to keep track of your passwords is through an online service, such as LastPass, which encrypts and stores your passwords.

Checking your credit report regularly is critical to early detection of identity theft. A credit report is a detailed record of what you owe and to whom, what you've paid, and if you've made any late payments to vendors. If you have an updated copy of your credit report, you will know if someone has hijacked your identity by taking out a credit card in your name. The Fair Credit Reporting Act requires each of the nationwide consumer reporting companies (Equifax, Experian, and TransUnion) to provide you with a free copy of your credit report, at your request, once every 12 months. Go to www.annualcreditreport.com to get your free report as soon as possible. To learn more about credit reports, be sure to read Chapter 1 – Check Your Credit Report Now!

Taking these simple steps to protect your identity now could save you a lot of time, money, and anxiety in the future. A half hour spent setting up a firewall, increasing the security on your passwords and PINs, and ordering a free credit report will decrease your chances of becoming one of the millions of identity theft victims.

## Signs you may be the victim of identity theft

- Missing bills
- Being denied credit for no apparent reason
- Getting calls from debt collectors about unfamiliar bills
- Receiving medical records in your name that don't pertain to you

Source: www.ftc.gov

## What to do if you become a victim of identity theft

Maybe you get a phone call from a representative from your bank, asking about suspicious activity on your account. Maybe you notice a charge at a jewelry market in Mumbai when the closest you've gotten to India is ordering chapatti from the restaurant across the street. Maybe you're turned down for a credit card when the last time you checked—a year ago or so—your credit score was pristine. Even if you are diligent about preventing identity theft, it can happen.

Here's what OnGuard Online recommends you do if it happens to you:

**Place a fraud alert in your credit file.** This alerts potential creditors that your identity might be compromised and informs them to follow certain procedures to ensure whoever's trying to charge in your name is unable to do so. You can place a fraud alert by contacting any one of the three credit agencies: Experian (www.experian.com), TransUnion (www.transunion.com), and Equifax (www.equifax.com).

**Close any affected accounts.** Report the issue to the correct department, then follow up with a written letter. Keep track of all communication about the issue: Take notes on phone conversations you have with representatives and file email and written correspondence.

**File a police report.** Having the theft documented by local police will help you recover your losses.

**Report your theft to the Federal Trade Commission.** Your report could help the FTC and the various law agencies nab the thieves and it will certainly help you recover your losses more quickly. You may file your report online at www.ftc.gov or call the hotline at 1-877-ID-THEFT.

We'll wrap up this chapter with a little quiz and a reminder. What do Target and the U.S. Department of Veterans Affairs have in common? Both of them exposed millions of people's personal information through security breaches. Target's systems were hacked, leaving 40 million customers' credit and debit card information exposed; the Department of Veterans Affairs recycled a hard drive containing unencrypted personal information of tens of millions of veterans. The reminder? Do what you can to prevent yourself from exposing your personal information to identity thieves—and check your credit report regularly just in case another company or organization has accidentally exposed you.

# BANKING

## CHAPTER 13

Step right up and get a free phone! A free iPad! $100! $200! Check out our giant inflatable piggy bank! Sign up for our Valentine's Day special!

Ever get the feeling banks really want your business? Let's see…you need a bank, they need customers. It's a win-win situation, right?

Right. Except that banks are in the business of making money and you'll want to choose a bank that doesn't make too much money off of you. Consider this: the average checking account costs over $200 annually. Free checking is no exception, as the fees for ATM and teller use, automatic bill payment, check writing, and overdrafts mount up. Suddenly, those free phones, free iPads, cash rewards, and free balloons seem a little less attractive.

We know one woman who was shocked when she added up all the fees she had paid her bank in one year—and realized it was over $800! (If you already have a bank account, it might be interesting to go through your statements and add up all the avoidable fees.)

Of course, you need a bank. It doesn't make sense to hoard and hide your cash. You just need to choose—and use—your bank wisely.

## Common banking mistakes

Sometimes it just makes sense to start with what not to do. Here are some of the most common banking mistakes—if you can avoid them from the outset you'll save yourself a lot of money over the years:

**Keeping too much money in no-interest or low-interest bearing checking accounts.** Instead, keep just enough money in these accounts to pay bills on time and have adequate spending money. Put the rest in a higher interest bearing account. If you need to keep your funds liquid and reasonably accessible, investigate money market accounts that include check-writing privileges. And see Chapter 14 on Investing for more information on what to do with your excess money.

**Assuming online banking is unsafe and/or hard to use**. Quite the opposite. If you can use a computer, you can figure out how to bank online. Also, there are rarely fees associated with online banking. As far as cyber-security goes, as long as you practice proper "computer hygiene," such as guarding your password, investing in virus and firewall protection, as well as NOT checking the "remember me on this computer" box when using your computer, you don't need to be afraid of online banking.

**Focusing on one particular aspect of a bank's offers** – like free checking – and failing to examine the entire package the bank offers. Check out the whole picture. Often free checking promotions are masking higher fees/penalties elsewhere that will quickly erode any savings you get from free checking.

**Thinking a bank needs to be physically close to one's home or office.** Most people now use ATMs and checks for their banking transactions. In addition, banking services such as certified checks, deposits and money orders can be managed either electronically or by phone. When you do have paper checks to deposit, they can be submitted electronically by computer or smart phone, mailed or deposited at an ATM. If you live or work in an urban area that has banks on every corner, you are likely to be happy with a bank that is located near you. But if there are few banks in your area, don't hesitate to explore more distant options for better deals.

**Believing that changing banks is a difficult and painful process.** This process does take some organization and attention to detail, but if another bank is offering a better deal – lower fees and free checking – go for it. These small savings can really add up over time.

## Choosing a bank

You have three main choices: a bank with physical locations, an online bank, or a credit union. Banks and credit unions offer similar services and are almost all FDIC insured. However, they differ in whom they serve and how they do business. Banks want to make a profit, and do so by charging service fees and offering low interest rates on deposits. Credit unions, on the other hand, are nonprofit and owned by the members they serve. Their business model allows them to offer services at a much lower cost and to provide higher rates on deposits. However, credit unions are not open to everybody, they usually have a limited number of branches and a smaller network of ATMs, and they tend to offer a limited range of services. If you are eligible to join a credit union, it may be a good choice for you, but make sure you consider all potential costs before you make a decision.

**$20 ATM fees?**

If you use another bank's ATM, you may be charged $3, $5, even $20!

Traditional banks with physical branches are the most common option. Most traditional banks will offer a standard checking account that has low to no monthly maintenance fee. They count on the fact that people will rack up fees that offset the free checking. (Every bank has different fees, but some common ones to be aware of include fees for dipping below the minimum monthly balance, bouncing a check, or using a non-affiliated ATM.) Traditional banks generally have online banking services so you can do most of your banking from the comfort of, well, anywhere.

Online banks are another option. They usually offer free or low-cost checking accounts and services, and may have better interest rates than traditional banks. Some even offer no-fee ATM use at any ATM, which can be a bonus when you're out on the town or when you travel home for breaks. They have fees for overdrafts and non-sufficient funds and the like, of course. One downside of choosing an

**Consider This…**

## A very expensive day...

If your bank assesses an overdraft fee for each transaction—and many do—one overdrawn day could get very expensive! Consider this hypothetical situation: Your bank account hits zero and you don't realize it. You proceed to use your debit card to buy some groceries, fill up your gas tank, and get a soft serve cone at the drive-in. If your bank charges a $30 overdraft fee, you'll have to pay $90 for those three transactions!

online bank is that it may be inconvenient to make deposits. You may have to set up automatic deposits or send the checks to them in the mail, though some banks offer convenient at-home deposit options where you can submit a deposit using your smartphone.

## What do you need from a bank?

Evaluate your banking needs before you make a decision. Review your previous banking habits, as well as your current situation. Consider where you will live throughout the year and what kind of banking you think you will need. Be realistic about your banking habits and needs.

Ask yourself…

How many checks will I need to write a month?

- How many ATM withdrawals will I want to make per month?
- What kind of minimum monthly balance—if any—can I count on maintaining?
- What are my online banking needs and preferences?
- Do I ever overdraw my account?
- Do I want to earn interest on my deposits?
- Will my primary banking be done online or at the bank branch?
- Do I tend to keep track of my account balance?

Once you figure out how you're likely to use a bank, consider the options available to you. Here are some items you can evaluate in order to comparison shop:

- Interest rates
- Online banking features
- Number and location of ATMs
- ATM fees
- Deposit options
- Loan services
- Credit card/Debit card services
- Bill pay options
- Certificates of Deposit (CDs)

- Federal Deposit Insurance
- Fees and requirements
- Alerts and protection against fraud
- Money Market Accounts (MMAs)
- Convenience of locations
- Overdraft protection
- Brokerage services
- Reward points for credit card or debit card use

Compare each bank's fees, as well. Here are some of the most common fees to watch out for:

- Overdraft fees
- Excessive withdrawal fee
- Bounced check fees
- Low balance fee

- Out-of-network ATM charges
- Wire transfer fees
- Electronic bill payment fee
- Check printing charges

- Charges for teller service
- Check processing fees
- Money order fees
- Certified check fees

Take your time to comparison shop. Offers like "Open an account and get $250!" and "Get Free Checking!" are tempting, but in the long run they might not work out for you. When you've decided on a bank, you may open an account in person, online, or by mail. You will probably need two pieces of identification and an address.

## Tips to help you save

Banks and credit unions collected nearly $32 billion in overdraft fees in 2012. The banking profession might be known for being staid and boring, but bankers are ultra-creative when it comes to fees. Charges for everything from overseas transactions to ATM use have been rising steadily every year, and if you're not careful you might end up paying hundreds of dollars annually in avoidable fees. Here are some tips:

**Know what part of "free" means "fee."** Sure, your bank will charge fees for some services. If you know what they are you can avoid getting stuck paying for them.

**Use direct deposit.** Many banks will waive certain fees if you use direct deposit. If your employers offer direct deposit, sign up for it.

**Maintain a minimum balance.** Banks calculate your minimum balance in one of two ways: daily minimum balance, which requires you to maintain the balance every single day, and average daily balance, which requires you to maintain the balance as an overage over the billing cycle. Make sure you choose a realistic balance option—if you have a choice between the two—and maintain the balance required by your bank.

**Opt in for overdraft protection.** Sometimes things happen that are beyond your control. For example, you might write a series of checks and then realize your paycheck was never deposited. With overdraft protection, banks advance you the money to cover the checks you have written. There are usually fees for this service. Know what your bank's policy and procedures are and how much overdrafts might end up costing you.

**Ask for discounts and waived fees.** Once your bank has you as a customer, they want to keep you. Don't be shy about asking your bank for a better deal or to waive certain fees.

**Don't order checks from your bank.** Most banks charge between $12 and $17 for a box of 250 checks. A cheaper option is to order checks directly from the check-printing company. Find these companies online.

**Use online bill pay options.** You'll save on stamps and checks. Also, you can set up automatic payments so you won't get stuck paying the fees vendors charge for late payments.

**Know where your bank's no-fee ATMs are located.** If you use ATMs that are not part of your bank's system, you will be charged an average of $2.60 per transaction, according to Bankrate.com's most recent survey of checking accounts. Often, you will be charged twice: once by your bank and again by the ATM company.

**Request cash when you use your debit card to make purchases.** Most banks don't charge fees for "cash back" transactions. If your bank charges you for debit card transactions, consider switching banks.

**Limit transactions and bank visits** if your checking account has a maximum number of such services allowed per month. However, it's important to note that there are so many banking options available that you shouldn't have to settle for a bank that limits transactions and bank visits.

## Online banking

Even if you don't choose to open an account with an online bank, you'll probably do a fair amount of online banking. Online banking can be a safe, secure and convenient alternative to traditional banking. However, keep in mind that online banking, like any online transaction, is only as safe as you make it. Therefore, protect your password, invest in virus and firewall protection, and never use the "Remember Me" function on your computer.

Banks are more than eager to get their customers to use their online services because it is extremely cost-effective for them. In fact, they will often give their customers incentives for using this service, like waiving normal maintenance fees or raising limits on the number of transactions you can make.

It's cost effective for you, too. Fewer trips to the bank means you have more free time and spend less on gas. In addition, immediate online access to your account allows you to spot and deal with trouble as soon as it happens.

One of the best aspects of online banking, besides direct deposit, is the ability to pay your bills online or through automatic debit. Doing so saves time, postage and check costs, and automatically provides an electronic record of payment. Bear in mind that there is lag time between when you pay the bill electronically and when the vendor receives payment. Therefore, do not wait until the due date to pay the bill. As a general rule, you should pay a bill online at least six business days before the due date. If you are solvent and your life is predictable, you often can arrange for a vendor to automatically deduct your payment each month from your checking account. However, do NOT do this if you run the risk of overdrafts.

## Keep track of your account

If someone offered to pay you $200 to balance their accounts correctly, would you do it? When you balance your own account and avoid costly mistakes like overdrafts and additional fees, you get to keep more of your money. Here are some ways to manage your account without making it a full-time job:

- Keep track of debit card purchases and ATM transactions in a register

- Use duplicate checks so you have copies for your reference

- Note when you make deposits and when the funds will be available

- Keep receipts for purchases, withdrawals, and deposits

- Establish a regular time each week to review your accounts and update any activities you may have forgotten

- Set up your online banking so you can check your account balances and recent activity

- Read the notices your bank sends you

- File your records so you can find them easily at tax time

It's important to check your account balance regularly. Doing so will help you avoid any surprises that can crop up, such as an overdrawn account or a faulty deposit.

### Managing Online Accounts

Research online money tracking sites that can help you manage your account. Some of them categorize expenses, send alerts when funds are low, and help you visualize your cash flow with handy charts and graphs. Your bank probably offers such online services. If they don't, research online or check out money tracking sites like Mint.com and Yodlee.com.

You might find that the best bank for you is the one that's offering that iPhone promotion. If so, great! Go for it. If you've done your homework you'll know when you've made the right decision. Equally, if not more, important are the daily decisions you'll make that can help you avoid fees and keep track of your money. Ideally, your money will be working for you, earning interest. If you're not quite to the point where you have enough money to earn interest, you can do the second best thing: make sure you're not losing the money that you do have to unnecessary fees and mistakes.

# INVESTING

## CHAPTER 14

You are already an investor, even if you don't know the difference between a U.S. Treasury bond and a bon-bon. (Treasury bonds are investments backed by the United States government; bon-bons are small chocolate-covered confections.) You invested your time, energy, and money into a college education, for example. When you buy a piece of sports equipment, you are investing in your health and quality of life. Hey, when you buy a bon-bon, you are investing in a small pleasure. Are these wise investments? Maybe, maybe not. If the surfboard simply sits in the storage unit year after year, you're not getting a very good return on that particular investment. The point is, even if you are not Warren Buffett, you are an investor: you invest time, energy, and dollars into all sorts of things every day.

Many people are intimidated by financial investing because they see it as complex, requiring years of study or a lot of money. But the purpose of financial investing is simple: to build wealth. And while it can be quite complex and involved, you can also keep it simple and start small. As little as $50 or $100 per month will get you started.

Consider this scenario: It's 1986. Our protagonist, Josh, receives $220 from his grandparents for his 10th birthday. He's torn about how to spend the money. There's a new pair of acid-washed jeans and a leather bomber jacket at the mall that he's had his eye on. Or he could invest the money in stock and buy 10 shares in that company he's heard about. You know the one: Microsoft. Josh's 10 shares—if he had purchased them and held on to them—would have been worth $72,000 in 2011 on the 25th anniversary of that company's IPO. Instead, he invested in his future children's entertainment: they love laughing at the photos of dad in his acid-washed jeans and bomber jacket.

Of course, Josh could just have easily invested his $220 in a company that tanked. Then he'd be without a cool outfit *and* without the money. Investing does involve risk, after all. This chapter will provide you with a basic understanding of investing – what it is and isn't, some guidelines on how to determine your tolerance for risk, and a description of the common investment options available to you.

## What's your money doing?

Let's say you put a crisp $100 bill in a drawer in the year 2004 and you didn't do anything with it until the year 2014. When you pulled it out in 2014, it would still be green and crisp and have the number 100 on it—but you would have lost the equivalent of about $31. Inflation marches on, things cost more every year, and the money that we keep hanging around in drawers, under mattresses, and in low-interest bearing bank accounts, is chipped away by time.

A few years ago, a hedge fund manager in New York accidentally left an ATM machine without claiming his receipt, which showed a savings account balance of almost $100,000,000. The news wires picked up the story and people all over the country were shocked. Many people were shocked that one person could have so much money. Financial types were shocked for a different reason: What was the guy doing keeping his money in a *savings account!?!* He might as well have been throwing a little out every day, since a typical savings account does keep pace with inflation.

> Check out the inflation calculator at
> http://www.bls.gov/cpi/
> *TIP*

As you can see, the words "saving" and "investing," while often used interchangeably, are very different.

## Saving

Savings are dollars you've put aside for emergencies or for very specific purposes. Therefore, you need a safe place to keep them. Savings accounts and other low-yield accounts are ideal for savings. When you save, you want the money to be "liquid," there when you need it. You don't have to sell anything or wait to get your money: You go to the bank or other financial institutions, ask them for your money, and they give it to you.

You earn interest on savings, but it's not really an investment. Savings accounts are very safe (*low risk*) and don't yield much return—interest-bearing checking and/or savings accounts pay as little as 1% annually—and some even charge you a maintenance fee. Money market accounts (*a form of savings account*) have slightly higher yields, but generally require you to meet certain requirements to qualify for those yields.

Remember that crisp $100 bill? If you had put it into a savings account in the year 2004 and that account earned 1% interest, you would have a little over $111 when you checked on it in the year 2014. Great! It earned money, right? Kind of. You have more money in the account than when you started, but the money did not keep up with inflation, which has averaged 3.22% from 1914 – 2013.

## Investing

Investing is about increasing your net worth, and about meeting long-term financial goals. It involves more risk (*possible loss of money*) than saving, but provides more rewards (*possible greater yield*) as well. If you had invested that crisp $100 in the year 2004 into a fund that earned 7% compounded interest you'd have $210 by 2014. (Of course, in that particular period of time, you were probably more likely to lose money; however, historically the stock market has yielded about 11% interest.)

## Are you ready to start investing?

Perhaps. If you can answer "yes" to the following questions, then you are in a position to start investing. If you answer "no" to any of them, you'd be wise to wait.

**Do you have an emergency fund of at least three months' living expenses?** You need this much set aside so you won't have to sell your investments to get through something like the loss of a job or a serious illness. A three-month cushion (some suggest at least six months) will see you through most emergencies.

**Do you have adequate insurance?** Not having adequate insurance could lead to financial disaster, so it should take priority over financial investing.

**Do you have no credit card or other high-interest debt?** If you're carrying any credit card debt, the best investment you can make is to pay them off! It will do you no good to have investments yielding 8% if you're spending more than that to service high-interest debt.

**Are you maximizing your retirement options such as your 401(k) or other opportunities?** Take full advantage of any matching funds available to you. None of the investment choices you'll find out about in this chapter will return that much.

**Do you have a budget that you follow?** When you maintain a budget, you'll know exactly how you spend your money and how much you can afford to invest.

How did you do? If you answered yes to all of these questions, you have a lot to be proud of. And a lot to look forward to.

## What do you need to start investing?

If you meet the criteria outlined in the previous section, your next step is to determine how much money you can and want to invest. You don't need a lot of money to start investing – you just need to start! If you have as little as $50 a month available, you can start investing.

Two myths about investing:

- **You need a lot of money to invest.** Not so. For example, most mutual funds require a minimum investment of $2,000 to $3,000. However, some will allow you to open a fund with as little as $50 if you agree to have that amount automatically deposited monthly from your checking account. But mutual funds are not your only option; there are many other investment options you can participate in with a minimal monthly contribution. (We'll explain more later in the chapter.)

- **You need to pay a financial advisor to help you invest**. A lot of investments can be purchased without consulting a financial advisor. In fact, self-directed investing is very common. You just need to do some research, then check out the various online investing opportunities.

The truth is that investors generally start out small – especially when they're young. The great thing about investing when you're young is that you have the luxury of time – time to watch your little investment grow.

## How much risk can you tolerate?

Risk, as it relates to investing, is the possibility that you could lose some or all of your money. Investing isn't exactly like gambling, but you can lose your initial investment all the same. What is your risk tolerance? Assume that you have $1,000 to invest for 12 months. If losing 5 percent of that money, or $50, is the most you would be willing to lose, then you probably have a low risk tolerance. If, on the other hand, you would be okay with losing 25 percent, or $250, count yourself as a moderate risk-taker. If the thought of blowing as much as 40 percent ($400) of your initial $1,000 isn't all that troubling, you likely have a high-risk tolerance.

| IF YOU HAVE | AND COULD TOLERATE LOSING | YOU'RE A |
|---|---|---|
| $1000 to invest | 5% or $50 | Low-risk Investor |
| $1000 to invest | 25% or $250 | Moderate-risk Investor |
| $1000 to invest | 40% or $400 | High-risk Investor |

Do the same calculations, only this time up the initial investment to $10,000. What's your risk tolerance now? 5 percent ($500)? 25 percent ($2,500)? 40 percent ($4,000)? Your risk profile will change depending on the amount of money you invest, your investment goals, and the circumstances of your life.

## When do you want to use your investments?

Your goals and when you want to reach them will impact your risk profile. Let's say you're planning your wedding for two years from now. You'll need to put the money you've invested to pay for the wedding in something relatively safe. However, for something further out on your timeline, a moderate risk strategy is appropriate. For longer-term goals, such as building your dream house, a higher-risk investment might be the right choice. Remember, the higher the risk, the higher the potential reward. What you want to do is strike a balance between wildcat, go-for-broke high-risk investing and ho-hum investing by finding investments that will accumulate wealth and still let you sleep at night.

Retirement might take a completely different strategy. The Securities and Exchange Commission (SEC) suggests that if your investment horizon, or the amount of time you have to let your money accumulate wealth, is long – say 35 or 40 years until retirement – you might consider more risky investments. Why? Because less risky investments may grow too slowly to keep up with inflation.

## What are your investment options?

The most common investment categories include cash, bonds, stocks, and mutual funds. Each of these categories includes a variety of options.

### 1. Cash

As mentioned earlier, cash is a form of savings. However, when developing an overall investment plan, it's important to understand what savings options are available to you. Following is a list of common cash savings options.

**Savings Account** Savings accounts are usually offered by financial institutions, such as banks, and offer a very low rate of return. Money usually can be withdrawn without penalties.

**Certificates Of Deposit (CDs)** CDs are a specialized deposit that can be purchased from a financial institution such as a bank or credit union. A CD is a loan you make to a financial institution over a certain time period. Most CDs provide annual interest payments during the life of the CD and will return the original invested amount plus interest when the CD expires.

CDs often offer a higher rate of return than savings accounts because of the time requirement involved. However, you should be aware that if you withdraw money from a CD prior to its maturity, you will be assessed a fee for early withdrawal, so you need to be sure you can live without that money for the life of the CD.

**Money Market Account (MMA)** Money market accounts are invested primarily in short-term and high-quality bonds, treasury bills, and CDs. They usually offer returns higher than a savings account, but lower than a CD. The advantage of money market accounts is the ability to withdraw money without penalty. Some money market accounts are now insured up to a certain dollar amount. Prior to investing, determine if the money market account is insured and up to what limit.

## 2. Bonds

A bond is an IOU promised by the United States government (*treasury bonds, savings bonds*), federal agencies, state and local governments (*municipal bonds*), and corporations (*corporate bonds*). In return for your loan, the creator of the bond promises to pay you a specified rate of interest during the life of the bond in addition to repaying the entire value of the bond when the bond matures.

Bonds, just like other forms of investments, include several options based on the amount of risk you're willing to accept. The great thing about bonds is that a rating system has been developed to determine the amount of risk associated with a bond. A bond that is rated triple-A (*AAA*) is usually safer than a bond that is rated double-B (*BB*). However, the AAA bond will usually have a smaller rate of return than the BB bond. Bond ratings are available from several resources, such as the Internet, financial institutions, and newspapers. Below are descriptions of the various forms of bonds.

**Treasury Notes and Bonds** The U.S. Treasury issues treasury notes (*2 to 10 year maturity*) and treasury bonds (*10 to 30 year maturity*). These investments are backed by the "full faith and credit" of the United States government and thus are considered low risk.

**Municipal Bonds** Bonds issued by states and municipalities to finance public projects, such as roads, schools, and hospitals are municipal bonds. One benefit of municipal bonds is that they may be tax-exempt from federal and state taxes.

**Corporate Bonds** Occasionally corporations need to borrow money for long-term projects. Instead of issuing more shares of ownership (*stock*) to raise funds, a corporation will issue bonds. The risk associated with bonds will vary depending on the history and financial stability of the company offering the bond.

## 3. Stocks

A stock is a unit of ownership in a corporation that you receive in the form of a piece of paper. The ownership of a stock entitles you to participate in various decision-making matters, such as the election of a company's directors or the sale of additional shares of company stock. By purchasing a share of the company, you are accepting the possibility that the company's value may increase or decrease. This increase or decrease in value will be reflected in the company's stock price.

In addition to the increase or decrease in a company's stock price, some corporations offer their shareholders dividends. Dividends are payments of the company's profits that are not invested in the company. Dividends are most common in very large, low risk, and financially stable companies. Once you purchase stock in a company, you may be able to purchase additional shares of the company's stock with dividend payments. This is known as a dividend reinvestment plan. This lets you obtain more shares in the company while avoiding fees usually associated with purchasing additional shares.

With some exceptions, there is no mandatory length of time you must retain ownership of stock. However, stock tends to be a long-term investment. In addition, the fees associated with the purchase and sale of shares of stock typically make frequent purchases and sales cost-prohibitive.

Following are brief descriptions of the various types of stocks:

**Large-Cap Stocks** Stocks offered by large companies, such as automobile manufacturers and utility companies, are known as large-cap stocks or "blue chip" stocks. These shares generally have limited growth prospects, and investments in these companies are usually suited for long-term investment horizons. Although the stock price may remain relatively stable, these companies offer the largest dividends.

**Mid-Cap Stocks** Stocks offered by mid-sized companies, such as regional grocery chains, are known as mid-cap stocks. These shares generally have good growth prospects and tend to re-invest profits. Therefore, dividends are rarely offered by these companies.

**Small-Cap Stocks** Stocks offered by small companies, such as start-up technology companies, are known as small-cap stocks. These stocks tend to have good growth prospects, but may be based on unproven (*non-stable*) products or services. Therefore, the risk associated with these stocks is quite high. Because these companies are interested in building up their business, profits are almost always re-invested and never paid out as dividends.

## 4. Mutual Funds

Mutual funds were developed as an investment tool to give investors the ability to pool their money together and invest in a variety of assets. Professional money managers buy, sell, and monitor the investments. This allows you to spread your funds and risk among many assets, which would otherwise be cost prohibitive.

To ensure that the mutual fund is invested in the proper assets that will maximize growth within a certain acceptable risk level, a manager is appointed. All mutual funds charge a fee for this management service. The size of the fee depends on the level of management involvement. Management fees are usually charged as a percentage of the value of your mutual fund. For example, you might be charged 2 percent of the value of the fund.

As with stock, the fees and expenses associated with buying and selling a mutual fund tends to make investing in a mutual fund a long-term investment decision. In addition to the fees and expenses, a longer time frame is needed in order to achieve the intended results.

Following are brief descriptions of the various forms of funds:

**Money Market Funds** Money market funds are invested primarily in short-term and high-quality bonds, treasury bills, and CDs. They usually offer returns higher than a savings account but lower than a CD. The advantage of a money market account is the ability to withdraw money without penalty.

**Bond Funds** As discussed earlier in this section, there are a variety of bonds available for purchase. Because of this variety, there are a number of options for mutual funds based on bonds. For example, you can have a corporate bond fund, municipal bond fund, or U.S. government fund.

**Stock Funds** There are a number of choices of mutual funds that invest in stocks:

- **Aggressive Growth Funds** – typically invest in small companies and are usually one of the highest-risk mutual funds. These companies almost always focus on growth and do not pay dividends.

- **Growth Funds** – typically invest in well-established companies that emphasize growth and usually pay small dividends.

- **Growth & Income Funds** – typically invest in firms that have some growth potential, but mostly focus on firms that consistently pay dividends.

- **Income (*Equity*) Funds** – typically invest in companies that pay dividends.

- **Global Funds** – typically invest in stocks of overseas companies as well as the United States.

- **International Funds** – typically invest strictly in stocks of overseas companies.

Set-up and management fees are commonly referred to as load and no-load funds. Below is a brief description of these fees:

**Load Fund** A load fund will charge either an up-front fee when the fund is purchased or a redemption fee when the fund is liquidated. For instance, if you have $1,000 to invest in a fund and the fund charges an up-front fee of 3 percent of your initial investment, $30 will be deducted from the $1,000 and the remaining $970 will be invested.

**No-Load Fund** A no-load fund will not charge up-front or redemption fees. However, many of these funds tend to charge for a variety of other services. Therefore, be sure all possible fees are explained to you before you agree to a no-load fund.

## Diversification

If you know the phrase "don't put all your eggs in one basket," then you know what diversification is. Because investments fluctuate, if you place your money in different investments with returns that are not completely correlated, when some of your investments are down in value, odds are that your other investments are up.

Diversification is one of the reasons mutual funds have become a good choice for investors. As mentioned before, mutual funds give you the ability to purchase a variety of different stocks, bonds, or cash equivalents. If you purchased one of these securities on your own, say stock in General Motors, your success or failure would depend solely on the performance of that individual stock. However, when you invest in a mutual fund, you are investing not only in General Motors, but also dozens or even hundreds of other companies. Thus, if General Motors' stock plummets, chances are the stock prices of all the other companies in your mutual fund will counteract the negative effects of the reduced value of General Motors' stock.

You may be thinking to yourself that in order to further diversify your investments, you should purchase a mutual fund in each of the different investment categories. For example, one in stocks, one in bonds, and one in cash equivalents. This would certainly diversify your investment portfolio. However, you would then have several different mutual funds to keep tabs on, plus you'd be paying management fees to each of these funds. To avoid this hassle and cost, mutual fund companies have created several individual funds that accomplish this for you – where the fund includes a mix of stocks, bonds and cash equivalents. Therefore, you achieve a diversified investment portfolio (in stocks, bonds and cash equivalents) with only one mutual fund.

## Asset allocation

Asset allocation is a term used to describe how you spread your money among different investment options (stocks, bonds, and cash equivalents). So how do you decide how much of your money should be allocated to stocks, how much to bonds, and how much to cash equivalents? The answer is dependent on a number of factors, including your present financial situation, your goals, and the risks associated with various investment options.

Most financial planners advise that you have at least three to six months of living expenses in cash equivalents in case of an emergency. Once you accomplish that, take the remaining amount of funds available for investing and allocate that to stocks and bonds. "How much of each?" you ask. A common (conservative) approach to asset allocation is to subtract your age from 100 and invest the resulting percentage in stocks. The remaining amount is invested in bonds. For example, if you're 23 years old, you would aim to invest 77 percent (100-23) in stocks and 23 percent in bonds.

Of course, this approach to asset allocation may not fit everyone's specific needs. If you are a moderate or high-risk investor, you may want to allocate more of your money to stocks. Again, this is a personal decision and is dependent on a number of factors. Do your research, consider the risks, and choose wisely.

## Which investments should you choose?

The sheer range of investment options may be overwhelming at first. The key is to determine what you would like to invest in, based on your goals, timeline, and risk tolerance, and then do some research. There are countless resources available on investing – everything from books, magazines, Web sites, television shows, investment companies, and financial planners. Use all of these resources, ask questions, and do more research. As you know, investing involves risk, and the more you know, the better equipped you are to evaluate that risk.

## Where should you purchase your investments?

There are literally thousands of companies that sell investments – banks, mutual fund companies, securities brokers, and even insurance companies all compete for your investment dollars. The companies you should look for are those that offer you valuable help without charging outrageous fees and those whose representatives have no self-interest in which investments you buy. Like always, research the various options to determine what is the best fit for you. Following are descriptions of a few of the common choices:

**Full-Service Broker** Full-service brokers are the middle person that takes your buy and sell orders and relays them to the market. In addition, full-service brokers give you advice regarding your personal financial planning. This planning will help you set goals, provide you with advice on investing, and help you develop timelines to meet your goals. Keep in mind that this "full-service" comes with a big fee. If you've done your own research, this is a service you probably don't need.

> Check out Brokers and Investment Advisors at the Security and Exchange Commission's website: http://www.sec.gov/investor/brokers.htm
>
> *TIP*

**Discount Broker** If you know exactly what investment you wish to purchase, a discount broker may be the way to go. A discount broker will take your buy and sell orders to the market; however, they do not provide any form of advice or financial planning services. Discount broker services can be accessed either in person, by telephone, or via the Internet.

**Internet** The Internet provides potential investors with a multitude of choices and information regarding investing. In addition, the Internet offers many investment services at significant discounts. However, be certain you are dealing with a legitimate company before transferring personal funds to them.

**Mutual Fund Company** Most mutual fund companies allow customers to purchase a mutual fund directly, thus bypassing the full-service and discount brokers. This method can provide cost savings depending on the type of mutual fund you purchase.

# TAXES

## CHAPTER 15

Taxes can be confusing, complicated, frustrating, and mysterious. They're hotly debated and the cause of national, state, local, and even household riffs. Everyone has an opinion about them, though tax code is notoriously difficult to understand. The humorist Dave Barry once claimed that the federal tax code is so big and scary that even IRS agents are afraid to get in the same room with it.

Over the years, the federal government has had to produce campaigns to inform the public about the hows and whys of income taxes, and the need to pay them on time. One WWII-era film short from the U.S. Treasury Department shows Donald Duck visiting Washington D.C. He resists paying his taxes, but the announcer intones, "This year, thanks to Hitler and Hirohito, taxes are higher than ever before…" By the end of the clip, Donald's convinced of his duty and hands the cash over. After all, how could anyone argue with a line like "Taxes defeat the Axis"?

Most of us don't refuse to pay our taxes, but we wonder, like Donald, where our money goes when we pay our taxes and what happens when it gets there. Every payday you will notice 30 to 40 percent of your paycheck has been culled for income taxes, FICA, and others.

This chapter will provide an overview of why and where your tax money goes and what it's being used for. It will also familiarize you with tax terms and provide some tips for reducing your tax burden.

In this chapter, we'll answer the most common tax questions.

## Why do we pay taxes?

As you may recall from the U.S. Government class you took back in high school, the role of our government is to provide for our defense, regulate commerce, establish justice, insure domestic tranquility, and promote the general welfare. To accomplish these tasks, the government requires funding. This funding is generated by the taxes you pay. You might say that taxes are the price we pay to live in a civilized society.

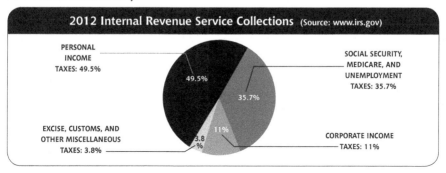

2012 Internal Revenue Service Collections (Source: www.irs.gov)

PERSONAL INCOME TAXES: 49.5%

SOCIAL SECURITY, MEDICARE, AND UNEMPLOYMENT TAXES: 35.7%

EXCISE, CUSTOMS, AND OTHER MISCELLANEOUS TAXES: 3.8%

CORPORATE INCOME TAXES: 11%

49.5%
35.7%
11%
3.8%

## What kinds of taxes do we pay?

You pay taxes on a lot of different things. Some you may be familiar with, and others you may not.

Following is a list of the most common taxes you pay.

- **Income Tax** – is a tax on your income. In addition to the federal government, some state and local governments also require you to pay income tax.

- **Sales tax** – is a tax on the stuff you buy and the services you use.

- **Property tax** – is a tax on applicable property, such as a home. Some states and local governments also apply property taxes to other forms of property, like a car, boat, or recreational vehicle.

- **Social Security and Medicare Tax** – commonly referred to as FICA, which means the Federal Insurance Contributions Act, this is a tax used to fund retirement income and health insurance to people 65 and over. In most cases you pay half of this tax and your employer is required to pay the other half. However, if you are self-employed, you are required to pay the entire amount. This is commonly referred to as the **Self-Employment Tax**.

## Who creates the taxes you pay?

When asked who creates the taxes you pay, most people answer the Internal Revenue Service (IRS). While the IRS is responsible for collecting taxes and enforcing tax law, it does not create the laws. Legislators and the President do.

Once legislators and the President pass a tax law, it is forwarded to the Department of the Treasury, which develops regulations on how the tax will be imposed, collected, etc. After that process is completed, the regulations are forwarded to the IRS, a bureau of the Department of Treasury. The IRS is then given the unpleasant task of enforcing the tax law.

Of course, not all taxes you pay are federal. Your local and state governments also impact the kinds of and amount of taxes you pay.

## Who decides how your tax dollars are spent?

Ultimately, it's you. You do this by choosing the politicians who will represent your interests in our government.

If you are unhappy with the level of taxation in your life, or you think your tax dollars can be better spent on more useful projects, then get involved. Understand where candidates for public office stand on taxes and how they believe those funds should be spent, and vote appropriately. Also, contact your legislators and let them know what you think the priorities should be. They have many interests vying for their time and attention; your voice should be among them. (Bookmark the website www.usa.gov, which is the portal to communicate with all of your legislators, state and federal.)

## How is your income tax calculated?

Unfortunately, there is no simple answer to explain how your income tax is calculated. It is an involved process that includes a number of variables, including your filing status, your taxable income, your applicable income tax brackets, and which deductions you are eligible to take. To assist you in understanding this process, each of these variables are explained in the following pages.

## Filing status

There are five different filing status groups. When you file your taxes you choose the group that most accurately describes your current situation. If your current situation makes you eligible for two of these groups, you should choose the one with the bigger deduction. The different groups include:

- **Single** – You are unmarried and do not qualify to file as Head of Household or Qualifying Widow(er).

- **Married, Filing Separately** – You are married as of the end of the tax year. You and your spouse each file a separate income tax return with your own income and deductions.

- **Married, Filing Jointly** – You combine your income and deductions with those of your spouse on the same tax return.

- **Head Of Household** – You are not married and you maintain a household for an individual who qualifies as a dependent.

- **Qualifying Widow(er)** – You may be able to use this filing status for two years after the year your spouse died, allowing you to use the rates as if you were filing jointly. Check the IRS website (www.irs.gov) for more details about qualifications for filing under this status.

## Taxable income

Determining your taxable income is a simple calculation. Unfortunately, the calculation involves a number of confusing terms. Therefore, before attempting the calculation, you should familiarize yourself with a few tax-related terms. These include:

- **Gross Income** – all the taxable income you earned throughout the year. This includes earned income (such as wages, sick pay, and unemployment) and unearned income (such as interest and dividends).

- **Adjustments** – the amounts you can subtract from your gross income. This includes items like IRA contributions, alimony payments, and moving expenses.

- **Adjusted Gross Income (AGI)** – your gross income minus adjustments.

- **Standard Deduction** – a reduction to your AGI for you, your spouse, and your qualifying dependents. These amounts are established by the government.

- **Itemized Deduction** – a reduction to your AGI for expenses like medical costs, mortgage interest, state and local taxes, employee business expenses, and charitable contributions.

- **Taxable Income** –the amount of income used to calculate your income tax.

- **Credit** - a direct dollar-for-dollar reduction of your income tax after it is computed on your taxable income. The Child Tax Credit is one example.

- **Witholding** – taxes that are taken out of your wages or other income before you receive them and that are deposited in an IRS account.

- **Estimated Payment** – quarterly tax payments you make to the IRS if your tax-withholding amount is inadequate. You may be required to make estimated tax payments if a significant amount of your income is not subject to withholding, such as net income from a business or investment income.

Now that you are familiar with these various tax-related terms, you are ready to calculate your taxable income, as well as your total income tax.

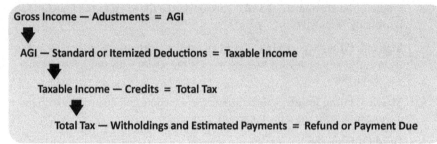

Gross Income — Adustments = AGI

AGI — Standard or Itemized Deductions = Taxable Income

Taxable Income — Credits = Total Tax

Total Tax — Witholdings and Estimated Payments = Refund or Payment Due

## Income tax brackets

In the previous calculation, you were able to determine how your total income tax is derived. However, the question of how much total income tax you owe still remains. How is that determined?

The United States uses a progressive tax system. With this system, taxable income levels are divided into brackets with lowest income brackets paying the least amount of tax. Tax brackets currently start at 10 percent and go to 35 percent. The more you earn, the more tax you pay. The chart provided below provides an excellent visual of the tax brackets used in 2013.

| Filing Status and Income Tax Rates 2013 | | | |
|---|---|---|---|
| Tax rate | Married filing jointly or Qualified Widow(er) | Single | Head of household | Married filing separately |
| 10% | $0 - $17,850 | $0 - 8,925 | $0 - $12,750 | $0 - $8,925 |
| 15% | $17,850 - $72,500 | $8,925 - $36,250 | $12,750 - $48,600 | $8,925 - $36,250 |
| 25% | $72,500 - $146,400 | $36,250 - $87,850 | $48,600 - $125,450 | $36,250 - $73,200 |
| 28% | $146,400 - $223,050 | $87,850 - $183,250 | $125,450- $203,150 | $73,200 - $111,525 |
| 33% | $223,050 - $398,350 | $183,250 - $398,350 | $203,150 - $398,350 | $111,525 - $199,175 |
| 35% | $398,350  - $450,000 | $398,350 - $400,000 | $398,350 - $425,000 | $199,175 - $225,000 |
| 39.6% | over $450,000 | over $400,000 | over $425,000 | over $225,000 |

So how does the progressive tax system work? Let's pretend for a moment that you were single in 2013 and you had a total income of $51,550. After adjustments, deductions, and credits, you had a taxable income of $41,550. Here's how your taxes would be figured if you were filing as a single taxpayer:

## Marginal and effective tax rates

At some time in your life you may have heard the terms marginal and effective tax rates thrown around, and wondered to yourself, "What are these and what do they mean to me?" Those are excellent questions.

**Marginal Tax Rate** is the rate applied on your last dollar of earnings. In the previous example, the marginal tax rate is 25 percent. Knowing your marginal rate will help you evaluate the value of making certain investment decisions. This will be discussed in more detail in the Investing chapter.

| Applicable Tax Brackets on $41,550 | Tax Owed |
|---|---|
| 10 percent tax on the first $8,925 | $893 |
| 15 percent tax on the next $27,325 | $4,099 |
| 25 percent tax on the last $5,300 | $1,324 |
| **Total Tax Owed** | **$6,316** |

**Effective Tax Rate** is the rate calculated by dividing the total tax paid by your total income. In the previous example, the total tax paid is $6,316 and the total income is $51,550. Therefore, the effective tax rate is 12.25%. Knowing your effective tax rate will also help you evaluate the value of making certain investment decisions, but for the most part, the effective tax rate is used simply to determine your overall tax burden.

Consider This ...

**During WWI, the top income tax rate was 77%!**

Source: www.irs.gov

## Reporting Your Taxes

Most people dread filing taxes, but if you go into the task prepared, it shouldn't cause much anguish. The first question is which of the four forms—1040EZ, 1040A and 1040—should you use? That will depend on your filing status, your income and the deductions and credits you have.

- **1040EZ** – Use this form if you are single, or married and filing jointly; have taxable income less than $100,000 and no itemized deductions.

- **1040A** – Use this form if you have income from several sources and your total income is less than $100,000. This form does not allow you to itemize, but does permit you to claim tax credits and take deductions for deductible IRA contributions and student loan interest.

- **1040** – Use this form if your itemized deductions are larger than the standard deduction, you receive income from a rental property or capital gains, or you own a small business.

If you filed a return last year, the IRS will happily send you a packet this year with the same form already in it. Unless your status has changed (for instance, you got a better paying job, got married, bought a house), you can continue to use the form they send.

Because tax law changes frequently, you should check with the IRS www.irs.gov to be sure you choose the correct form. Taxes are incredibly complex and so are the regulations that go with them. The IRS has a wealth of information on their Web site to help you.

## Reducing your tax burden

Regardless of your income level, you should consider creating a plan to take advantage of tax breaks written into the tax code. This is all legal and above-board. And there are a number of sound ways you can use the tax laws to keep more of your income.

**Tax-Exempt Investments** – With some investments, notably the Roth IRA, any money you earn is tax-exempt. This means you never have to pay taxes on it. Interest on Municipal Bonds is also generally tax-exempt.

**Tax-Deferred Investments** – Qualified 401(k) savings plans and IRAs allow you to make contributions, earn interest and dividends, but not pay the tax until you withdraw the money later in life. Theoretically, when you retire your tax bracket will be lower because you'll have less income, so any taxes you pay on money you withdraw from an IRA will be taxed at the lower rate. If you invest in securities that appreciate in value, you won't be taxed on that appreciation until and unless you sell those securities.

**Home Equity Loans** – Interest on most home equity loans, up to $100,000, is deductible. Interest on credit cards is not. Neither is interest on consumer loans. So, if you have credit card or consumer debt and equity in your home, you may want to consider taking out a home equity loan to pay down the debt – and deduct the interest from your gross income at tax time. Be sure that the home equity loan you apply for qualifies for tax a deduction before you sign anything.

**Paying Expenses with Pre-Tax Dollars** – Many employer health insurance plans offer flexible spending accounts (see Chapter 4, about insurance) that allow you to use pre-tax dollars for health care. Money is deducted from your paycheck before your withholding tax is taken out, thus reducing the amount of money on which your tax is calculated.

**Student Loan Interest** – If you have student loans, interest paid during the year is deductible if the loan was used for tuition, fees, room and board, supplies and other related items, and certain income limits must be met. Because limits change from year to year, you should check the IRS Web site for current information to determine if you qualify.

**Itemizing Deductions** - Itemizing deductions can reduce your AGI. However, be aware that rules for applicable deductions change every year. Be sure to read the information that comes with your IRS Tax Return package. Examples of itemized deductions include: State and local taxes; points paid on your mortgage; charitable contributions; home office expenses; job search expenses; moving expenses (if they're related to a new job); and gambling losses, but just up to the amount of gambling winnings.

## Keeping records

Good record keeping habits will make tax preparation much easier. You should keep all records you used to prepare your tax return for at least three years. But keep that tax return itself forever – it may save you a lot of trouble later.

Here's a list of some of the kinds of records you should keep and for how long.

| Type of Record | Keep It For |
| --- | --- |
| Annual Tax Return | Forever |
| Cancelled checks, bank deposit statements and receipts | At least 3 years, 7 years is better |
| Stock trade confirmation receipts/ statements | At least 3 years after both the buy and sell transactions have closed |
| Home improvements | At least 3 years after the sale of the property |
| Escrow closing documents | Minimum of 3 years after the property is sold |
| Tax preparation documents | 3 years minimum |

## Tax assistance

Resources are readily available to help you not only plan for your taxes, but prepare your return. You merely have to decide how much help you want. Following are some resources you might wish to consider.

**IRS** - The IRS (www.irs.gov) is the ultimate source of tax help. Their Web site is full of information to answer questions and direct you to helpful pages. If you prefer talking to a real person, a staff of IRS tax professionals is available to assist you by simply calling 800-829-1040.

**Tax Publications & Web Sites** – In addition to the publications produced by the IRS (available in print or online), there are a number of books and Web sites available that offer solid advice.

**Tax Preparation Software** – The fastest-growing method of filing a tax return is electronically. The IRS encourages electronic filing, which is both fast and free if you use the Web. Benefits of filing electronically are speed of filing, improved accuracy, and faster refunds.

To file electronically, you will need to prepare your taxes with IRS-approved tax preparation software – TurboTax and H & R Block's TaxCut are two of the more popular options. Advantages of using tax preparation software are:

- They are relatively inexpensive (*starting around $35*) and easy to use.

- You don't have to get forms; they're in the program.

- You can see what your tax liability is, and then make adjustments.

- The software prompts you with questions to help you take advantage of possible tax reductions.

- If you enter the information correctly, there is minimal chance for errors.

- The program carries information over to and enters it in all the required places. Plus, it does all calculations.

- Carryovers from year to year are automatic, assuming you use the same program each year.

However, there are some disadvantages to using tax preparation software. First, you have to trust the software. There's always a small chance that the software may have a flaw that can cause an error. In addition, if you're using an online service to file, there are always privacy concerns.

Be sure that the tax preparation software package you choose

> **E-filing: Easier and more accurate!**
>
> The error rate for a paper return is 21%. The error rate of an e-file return is just half a percent!
>
> Source: www.irs.gov
>
> *TIP*

includes state income tax forms, if that applies to your state. Also, if you purchase the software early, remember to get an updated version so you have the latest information and tax-code revisions.

**Professional Services** - If you simply want to load up all your records and have someone else complete the forms, there are a number of services available to assist you for a fee. These include storefront preparers (like H&R Block and Jackson Hewitt Tax Services), Certified Public Accountants, enrolled agents, and tax attorneys.

Before you head off to seek help from one of these tax professionals, be sure you have done your research. Determine what you will be charged for these services. Fees can be as low as $50 to as high as $300 per hour. You will also want to locate a service that is qualified to assist you. The more difficult your taxes are to prepare, the more qualified the service provider should be. Finally, ask friends, family or coworkers to recommend specific tax professionals they have used.

## Rapid refund offers

There are numerous tax preparation services offering customers "Rapid Refunds." Basically, this is a high-interest loan. You pay what appears to be a small fee, and in exchange your tax-preparer hands over your expected tax refund minus the fee.

Let's pretend for a moment that the IRS owed you $500. Instead of filing electronically and getting your money in two-weeks, you agree to pay a $34 fee for a "Rapid Refund." That rapid refund works out to an annual interest rate of over 200 percent. Yikes!!! And you thought an 18 percent interest rate on your credit card was bad. If you are ever offered a "Rapid Refund," take your tax return and run. You're about to be robbed!

If you could choose how much to pay in taxes and how those taxes would be allocated, how much would you pay? Where would you direct your tax dollars, if given the choice? Check out the calculator at www.wheredidmytaxdollarsgo.com. It will generate a pie chart based on information you plug in about your income and filing status. And, while you can't change the allocations on your own, you do have the power of voice and voting to let your legislators know how they can best represent you.

# INCREASE YOUR INCOME

## CHAPTER 16

The nip-and-tuck approach to finances—cutting coupons and eating rice and beans for every meal—only takes you so far. At some point, you just want to make more money. There are plenty of ways to increase your income, though not all of them are pleasant or legal. Some people take second jobs, start a side business, sign up to be medical test subjects at the local university, or sell their roommate's stuff on eBay. A better, often-overlooked way to make more money is simply to ask your boss for a raise.

## Why Request a Raise?

Consider This...

There's no guarantee that you'll be recognized and rewarded for your extra efforts in due time. You will probably have annual reviews and perhaps some cost-of-living adjustments, but you and your employer have naturally conflicting interests when it comes to your paycheck: You want to make more money and your employer wants to keep more money. Don't leave it up to your boss to raise the subject or up the ante.

When you take the initiative and approach your boss in a deliberate, rational way you'll end up miles ahead of where you'd be if you just waited.

We're not suggesting you march into your boss's office after a week on the job and declare it's high time for a pay increase. However, after you've been at your job for a year or so, reflect on where you are and what you're doing for the company. If you deserve a raise, ask for it, and get it, that little conversation with your boss could translate into a salary increase of several thousand dollars or more. And it would probably be less painful than enduring another sleep deprivation study at the local university or your best friend's wrath when he discovers his prized Pez dispenser collection has been sold on Craigslist and shipped off to Paduka.

Sure, you could get turned down if you request a raise. So? "No" is the second-best answer you could get. Don't jump in quite yet, though. Requesting a raise is a process that involves a lot of thought and preparation before you even make the appointment to talk with your boss.

## Do you deserve a raise?

This is the guiding question. We all want more money and can imagine everything we'd do with a plumped-up paycheck, but when you ask for increased

## Build a Personal File of Accomplishments

To Do!

Create a personal file filled with evidence of your accomplishments. Start it the first week on the job and add relevant pieces as you get them. What you're doing is compiling documentation that will prove (to yourself and your boss) that you are invaluable and working at a level worthy of higher compensation.

Include all evidence of your productivity, salesmanship, teamwork, customer and coworker relationships, problem-solving skills, etc.

The goal? To document compelling evidence of the value you contribute to the organization. This file can also come in handy if you need to transition suddenly to another job.

compensation you need to prove you really deserve it—first to yourself, then to your boss.

You deserve a raise if you…

- consistently exceed expectations
- have increased skills and education since you started the job
- perform significant duties beyond those outlined in your job description
- frequently work overtime in order to complete projects

When *you* are certain that you've performed at a level worthy of increased compensation, you'll be in a better position to sell your boss on the idea. The next step is to determine a fair salary for your work.

## How much are you worth?

You have unique, inherent qualities that make you a special being interconnected with the other beings of this planet. Unfortunately, you don't get a paycheck for any of that. Your "worth," as we're using the word here, is the amount your organization's willing and able to spend to employ you. Determining factors include your skills, education, and performance on the job, as well as organization, industry, and regional standards.

Figuring out fair compensation for your work takes algebraic grace and some research. Dig around to find out what others in your field are making. Good resources for expected salary range:

- Online salary calculators
- Professional organizations
- Your university's alumni and career services offices
- Want ads and on-line postings
- Your organization's human resources department
- Coworkers (be careful with this one!)

**Update Your Resume Regularly**

Even if you love your job and can envision yourself working there until you retire, treat it like it's one option among many. Update your resume every four months to stay sharp and focused on what you've already accomplished and what you want to achieve next. It doesn't need to be an official, perfectly-worded update. Handwritten notes will work just fine for this exercise.

What's the point? Updating your resume regularly allows you to reflect on the good work you're doing, the skills you've mastered, and what you need to do next in order to stay fresh and marketable. It also gives you the confidence to make a move—whether it's asking for a promotion or interviewing at another company—when you feel like it.

**How Much Should You Be Making?** Good To Know

There's no shortage of online salary calculators. Here are two that provide detailed information about comparable salaries— what other people with the same job title in the same region as you are making: www.salary.com or www.bls.gov

Don't dig too much with your coworkers. Be sensitive to the atmosphere of the office and your particular relationships with colleagues. Some companies are very open, but in most environments salaries are confidential and it's not OK to talk about them.

If you do have information about coworkers' salaries, do not bring that up in your negotiations. You'll prove your individual merit better if you don't make comparisons to others.

## Timing

So you've been at the job for a year, consistently do superior work, and have taken on more responsibilities. Is it a good time to ask for a raise? The answer is "yes" if...

- The organization seems to be on an up-swing: good earnings (if it's a publicly traded organization this will be easy to find out), lots of new hires, and no shortage of resources.

- You have recently impressed others with your creativity, sales, performance, etc.

- Headhunters or representatives from another organization have been wooing you.

- You are due for your annual performance review. Note: it's easier to negotiate an increase in the amount offered at a performance review than to request a meeting and review mid-cycle.

- The region's job market is strong.

### How Much Should I Ask For?

You'll get a barrage of wildly different responses to this question from negotiating experts. The national average for raises in the last few years is fairly low: 2 - 3%. Your human resources department might be willing to divulge the company average; this would give you a sense of precedent and expectations.

Some experts recommend you ask for double what you really want. Others suggest a more conservative approach (asking for 7% when you know you'd be happy with 5%, for example).

If your job duties are drastically different from when you were first hired or if you discover in your research that you're significantly undervalued, you might swing a hefty pay increase.

The answer is "maybe not" if...

- The company isn't doing well. Vacated desks, low earnings, rationed supplies, and negative news stories are all signs that it might not be the best time to ask for more money.

- You have recently made some mistakes or underperformed.

- The region's job market is weak.

Once you've determined that the company could probably afford to raise your pay (or that you're so good they can't afford *not* to), there's another bit of timing to consider: when to approach your boss. Schedule an appointment with him or her so that you'll have adequate time to present your case.

## How to be persuasive

Most of us mastered the art of persuasion by practicing on our parents. Let's travel back in time. You're in high school and you want something from your parents. No, not unconditional love or wise counsel. You want to borrow the car because you have a date. And you believe you'll improve your chances of having a successful evening if you drive your parents' car rather than asking your date to hop on the back of your tricked-out, low-rider bicycle. What makes for a "successful" evening? Well, that depends on your perspective, which matters very much to you but is not necessarily something you want to share with your parents.

The best approach to getting what you want in this scenario is to focus on your audience's—in this case your parents'—wants or needs. If you say, "Mom, I want the car tonight because it's gonna make me look hot and I need to look hot because I'm really hoping to impress my date and…", well, let's just say that Mom is not likely to be convinced.

Similarly, your boss doesn't want to know how a higher salary will help you afford a new car or pay off bills or take a trip to Europe. He or she wants to know how it will benefit the organization. Your task is to prove your value to him or her in a calm and reasonable manner, using documentation from your personal file of accomplishments. Always, always remember that this is not personal; it's business.

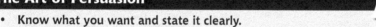

## The Art of Persuasion **TIP**

- Know what you want and state it clearly.
- Understand your audience: How will the boss and the organization benefit by giving you a raise?
- Support your argument with evidence. Provide documentation of accomplishments.
- Anticipate opposition and be prepared to counter it.
- Always maintain a calm, reasonable tone.

## And the answer is...

…usually not simple. You might get a resounding "Yes!" to your proposed increase, but it's more common to hear "Yes, if…" or "Maybe later…" or "Not right now…" or "How about this…." (Again, very similar to dealing with parents.)

This is why you prepared so much going into the meeting. You know what you want, why you're worth a higher salary, and what's at stake for you. What you are about to learn is what they can offer you. Maintain an open mind. Maybe the company can't afford the full amount you requested right now, but your boss is willing to let you telecommute twice a week or can offer you some other flexible work arrangement.

### The Line in the Sand

Be willing to back up everything you say. If you declare an ultimatum—*If I don't get this raise, I'm walking*—you have to be able to follow through on it. If you have other equally or more attractive options than your current job, then you're in a better bargaining position and can take more risks. However, if you're fairly happy at the company or don't have other viable options, keep the stakes lower.

**Consider This ...**

Sometimes bosses will counter a raise request with a slight pay increase and a new title; that might be a good option if you're thinking of moving on in the near future as it will show well on your resume.

Work with your boss to devise a plan to develop your expertise and improve your credentials so that you can move up in the organization or at least move up on the salary schedule. The best employer-employee relationships are mutually beneficial.

Salary negotiations can get complicated and confusing, so always be ready to say, "This is a lot to think about. I'd like some time to go over these ideas on my own. Can we meet tomorrow to talk about this some more?"

Negotiating is part art, part science, and part poker. Do everything in your power to demonstrate excellence on the job, document it, and then calculate what that's worth to you and your employer. Successful negotiations depend on being able to read the company climate as well as your particular audience, your boss. Then, of course, there's the leap: Declaring what you want and waiting for the reaction. Sure, there's a risk. But if you keep your cool during the process, there's little to lose and a lot to gain.

# MAKING A GREAT FIRST IMPRESSION

## CHAPTER 17

Ten seconds. That's about how much time you have to make a lasting first impression. (It's actually a little less time than that, but we'll round it up to simplify things.) Whether you're on a date, at an interview, or on day one of a new job, those first ten seconds have to be good. No biggie, right? Just enroll in some acting classes, hire a vocal coach, and convince some cheery talk show host to treat you to a total wardrobe makeover.

Here's the part where your blood pressure skyrockets while we tell you why humans are wired to make snap judgments and how it's really a good thing, a survival tactic we carry with us from the cave to the cubicle. Imagine, after all, the poor caveman who carefully deliberated, weighing the pros and cons of taking action when confronted by a charging bear. There are benefits to the quick appraisal: It saves time and energy. Also, our instincts are pretty reliable. We have inherent expertise that tells us, "Shifty eyes plus muttering plus clenched fists: bad. Nice eyes plus clear voice plus smile: very, very good." We don't have to take a body language seminar to know who's a potential threat and who's a potential mate.

Great, you say. Love the snap judgment when appraising, but it's a little nerve wracking to be the appraised. Plus, all this talk of bears and clenched fists raises the anxiety level a few notches. OK, relax. Because here's the part where we tell you what you can do to ensure you do make a great first impression on your new bosses and coworkers. And it doesn't involve a vocal coach or a total wardrobe makeover.

It does, however, mean debunking some favorite sayings, such as "Looks aren't everything" and "It's what's inside that counts." Yes, yes, but…the truth is that people judge on appearances first, then on personality and performance. So we have to pay attention to how we look and the impression we create.

## Grooming and dress

Grooming and dress are the first things people notice about you, long before they know anything about your work ethic or crystalline brilliance. Luckily, it's fairly easy to manage this aspect of your image and it doesn't necessarily have to cost your first year's salary.

For any job, you'll want to present a well-groomed, well-shod self. There are exceptions to these basic rules in some companies, where employees take the looks-aren't-everything maxim to heart and are often spotted coming to work in what might best be termed "pajama casual." In most companies, however, the norm now is definitely a professional or laid-back professional (otherwise known as "business casual") look.

## What's Your Company's Image?

Your interview and first visits to the company will probably give you a strong sense of the company's image and how you will fit in with it. The three most common modes of dress in today's workplace are Professional, Business Casual, and Creative. The definitions and descriptions of these categories do vary by company and region, but this chart is a good starting place for understanding your workplace's image.

| Dress Mode | Definition | Environment |
|---|---|---|
| Professional | Suit or sport jacket with slacks/skirt Collared shirt Conservative accessories Tie (men) Hose (women) | Banking, law, medical, engineering, insurance, sales, management, and accounting |
| Business Casual | Slacks (cotton OK in some offices) Knee-length (or longer) skirt Collared shirt (including golf-style shirts) Tailored sweater Coordinated accessories Hose and closed-toed shoes (required in some business casual environments) | Technology, education, journalism, retail, government, human services, and science |
| Creative | Anything goes (within the norms of the company culture) | Marketing, arts, and design |

So what should you wear? In some workplaces the dress code is obvious and might even be outlined in the employee handbook. In other companies the rules might be less clear and you'll see people in pinstripe suits working alongside others in jeans and sneakers. Dress according to what you see around you. Pay particular attention to the people who hold similar positions to yours: They are your most reliable resource when you're trying to figure out the wardrobe norms of the organization.

Even in a relatively casual office environment, it's worth dressing up a bit for the first few months of a new job. This is not to say that you need to wear a three-piece suit if everyone around you is in Bermuda shorts and flip-flops. One lesson we all learned in the throes of fourth grade, after all, was that fitting in is important and maybe even evolutionarily advantageous. However, in the case of your new job, it's better to err a little on the conservative side: A quick study of the best-dressed employee can reveal how to fit in while still projecting earnestness and ambition.

Now let's talk about the ever nebulous "casual day." What evil but brilliant clothing marketer came up with this concept? It's ambiguous at best, a cruel and misleading conspiracy at worst. Most of us, after all, have two types of casual: Painting the Town Red and Painting the House. Neither of these constitutes the "casual" in casual day, though if you look around the office you might see some clothes that would fit in well at the nightclub or, on the other hand, paint-bespattered, torn shorts that are one washing away from the rag pile.

## How to Wear It

**TIP**

### Here are answers to your most common style questions:

**How should my suit fit?** The jacket sleeves should hit your wrist bone when your arms are relaxed. About ½ inch of shirt should show beyond that.

**What's the best blouse fit?** A good-fitting blouse will not pucker at the shoulders or chest. If it's a long-sleeved blouse it should hit your wrist bone.

**What's the best trouser length?** Pants should rest on the top of your shoes in front and go about ½ inch down in the back. This rule applies equally to men and women, though some pants are cropped by design.

**How many shirt buttons can I leave undone?** For men and women, leaving the top one or two buttons undone is generally acceptable.

**What color socks should I wear?** Match pants, not shoes. Remember that socks should not be visible unless you're sitting down.

**What's the best heel height?** Shoes with a 1 – 2 ½ inch heel are a safe bet. In some organizations, higher heels will be acceptable.

**Do I need to wear hose?** That depends on the organization. Bare legs and open-toed or peek-a-boo shoes are acceptable in many workplaces.

**What's the best tie length?** The bottom of your tie should hit the spot between the top and bottom of your belt.

**How should I accessorize?** Shoes and belt should match each other. Wear minimal jewelry.

**What's the best skirt length?** Skirts should be knee length or longer.

## How Not to Wear It

**GOOD TO KNOW**

Your company may have a liberal dress code—or no dress code at all—but there are some hard-and-fast rules to follow if you want to make a positive impression.

**Don't show too much skin.** Make sure your V-neck is not too deep. Keep that chest—manly or womanly—under wraps. Also, all clothing should fit well and not be tight or clingy.

**Don't come on strong.** Douse yourself in perfume or cologne and you could turn people off and/or prompt an allergic reaction. Keep jewelry tasteful.

**Don't let your clothes say too much.** Clothing with offensive, distasteful, or questionable slogans is best left in the back of the closet.

Casual day is ripe for confusion. Usually, it means to dress comfortably without the sloppiness afforded by truly comfortable clothes. So you can wear jeans, but not the holey ones. "Dressy" T-shirts are OK, too. Again, the best guide to what's really appropriate is to consider how higher ups and well-dressed colleagues interpret the dress code. And when meeting with clients, definitely take your look up a few notches.

## Maintaining a groomed workspace

Unlike the interview, your image now that you actually have the job is a product not just of how well you take care of yourself but also how well you take care of your space. The state of your desk, office, or cubicle (even your handbag and car, in some professions) factors into your overall impression on others.

There's no revelation here, just a reminder to keep things organized and clean, especially in those first few months when you're building others' opinions of and confidence in you. Spend time setting up your office or cubicle and clean out your wallet, handbag, and briefcase.

When it comes to decorating your workspace, keep this in mind: It's an extension of you, a "personalized public space," not a private space. Make it comfortable and personal. It's OK to show off your family and friends, but keep the party photos at home.

## Non-verbal communication

Body language accounts for about half of what we say, and therefore comprises a huge part of our image. Try the following exercises to model this point. Stand with your arms crossed in front of you and eyes directed down at the floor. Say, "I'm so happy to meet you" in a cheerful voice. Or, cock your head to one side, raise an eyebrow, smile, and say, "I'll take a look at the data."

You're sending out signals all over the place. Your actual words, of course, count for some of what you say. But the tone of voice and body language you employ are much more significant indicators of your meaning. The most frequently cited study on interpersonal communication states that body language and facial expressions when someone is expressing feelings and attitudes account for 55% of meaning, tone and quality of voice account for 38%, and the actual meaning of the words count for just 7%.

Eye contact, posture, fidgeting…all of these non-verbal cues can reinforce or sabotage what you verbalize. Be aware of what your body is saying. You might even want to spend some time in front of a mirror, evaluating your "neutral position" (the way you carry yourself most of the time, when you're not actively engaged in conversation).

Here are some attributes of "positive" and "negative" body language:

**"Positive" Body Language**
(Signals interest, confidence, enthusiasm, and/or approachability)

- Nods head
- Uses hand gestures for emphasis (excessive gestures may signal aggression, however)
- Has erect posture
- Smiles
- Blinks at a regular rate
- Body takes up space (stance, posture, and arm position say, "I belong here")
- Cocks head slightly (shows interest, but can be interpreted as confusion or flirtation)

### "Negative" Body Language
(Signals boredom, insecurity, annoyance, and/or aloofness)

- Pins arms to side or across chest
- Handshake is limp or overpoweringly strong
- Slumps or hunches over
- Frowns, grimaces, or clenches jaw
- Expressionless, blank face
- Blinks too fast or stares
- Body closed off (stance, posture, and arm position say, "I don't want to take up any space")
- Fidgets excessively
- Rolls eyes
- Yawns or sighs

While it's easy to adopt a professional wardrobe even if you've been living in workout wear for the last few years, it's challenging to makeover your body language. After all, you've had decades to adopt the unconscious quirks that make up your body language vocabulary. Also, your posture, expressions, and gestures are more indelibly you than a shirt or shoes, and can't—and shouldn't—be discarded willy-nilly.

A few adjustments, however, might help you in your professional life. If you tend to sit back with your arms crossed during meetings, you'll project disinterest and maybe even resistance to new ideas. Reminding yourself to sit upright and to lean forward a little when listening to others could project a radically different, and more successful, image. Just being more aware of your image will help you change it.

## Verbal communication

Of course, while nonverbal communication accounts for an enormous part of one's image, verbal communication is still important. The average person says thousands (sometimes even tens of thousands) of words a day. So what, exactly, are we saying?

The truth is that some people don't know what they're saying or how they're saying it. Yet, communication skills are not optional, a bonus accessory some professionals happen to have; they are vital for every professional. Your success on the job is inextricably linked to the way you communicate.

What's your communication style? Do you say what you mean? Do you say it effectively? What do you inadvertently communicate to others when you talk to them? Take stock of your verbal communication skills and polish them if necessary—you'll be glad you did.

Communication styles can be influenced by a variety of factors, such as culture, gender, personality, and education. Everyone has his or her own personal style. Of course, that style is also dependent on one's surroundings: You probably won't use the same tone and vocabulary around your supervisor as you do your good friends. Understanding your own style as well as the different types you might encounter in others will give you an advantage in communicating with a broad range of people and will help you communicate more clearly. Here are some elements to consider:

**Rate of speaking.** Do you speak rapid-fire or back-porch? If you speak too fast, you risk losing people and/or appearing insecure. If you speak too slowly, you risk boring people and/or appearing, well, slow. Confident people know that others will listen to them, so they don't rush through their sentences. Considerate people know that they are not the only ones with something important to say.

**Volume and clarity.** You have good ideas and the skills to put them into action, but no one will know this about you if you mumble or speak too softly. Speak clearly, enunciate, and project confidence.

If you're really serious about assessing your verbal communication style, the best thing to do is to watch a video of yourself interacting with others. Be objective as you view the "evidence." Try to notice, not judge, your "ums," "ahs," "likes," and other inadvertent conversation habits. Consider these questions: How much time do you give to other speakers? Do you interrupt frequently, sometimes, or not at all? Is your voice audible? How do you physically present yourself? Many people find watching themselves on video about as pleasant as appendicitis during rush hour traffic. If you can get past the initial discomfort you'll find it's an invaluable exercise.

Another helpful practice is asking a trusted friend or family member to give you some honest and constructive feedback. Or find a group like Toastmasters International (www.toastmasters.org) that will provide an opportunity to practice public speaking in a non-threatening environment. It's a big—and for some, scary—commitment, but when you think of it as an investment it becomes clear that a little time and self-reflection now will pay off big in the future.

## Email and Instant Messaging

**Tone.** Email and IM are so pervasive and easy we forget how artful some of the messages need to be. Word choice, punctuation, and capitalization (plus an emoticon or two, maybe) are the only clues your reader has to your tone. Before you write an email, think about how you can communicate this information best. Sometimes a phone call or face-to-face conversation is better. If you think an email message is the best method for the situation, do take the time to compose your messages. Also, pause before you send. And with emotional emails of any sort, pause for at least 24 hours.

**Face-to-Face vs. Electronic Communication.** A decade ago, it would have been unheard of for next-door employees to email each other. But now it's such a creeping norm that some companies have taken the radical step of announcing no email days in order to engage employees in more face-to-face interaction. Go with the norms of your organization, but remember that in-person communication is a great way to build real relationships.

**Privacy.** Ha. Privacy is SO early 20th century. Email only those things you'd feel comfortable posting on the staff room fridge. If your father likes to forward every off-color joke and visual that's ever circulated the Web, tell him in no uncertain terms that he needs to remove you from his contact list. Or he'll be supporting you for the rest of his life. IM is not as easy to track and monitor, but work is work, and it's best to save the personal material for home. In fact, many organizations have strict rules against using company technology for personal matters. Another thing to note: If you have a Facebook or Twitter account or blog, know that it will certainly be viewed by someone from your workplace.

## Relationships with colleagues

OK, so you're well dressed, perfectly postured and enunciating with the precision of a broadcaster on network news. Your desk looks like the cover photo of a lifestyle magazine. Now what? Well, now you've got to play well with others.

You have a budding relationship with your boss already, which will develop according to the natural dynamics of boss-underling relationships. But equally important are the relationships you build with other people in the company, whether it's your boss's boss, the human resource coordinator, or the receptionist. Once you've been hired the real scrutiny begins, because your new coworkers have their chance to size you up. As the newbie in the office, you will fill several functions in addition to the official duties of your new job: stranger, rookie and, sometimes, source of entertainment. Anxious yet?

No problem. Yes, the first 10 seconds are critical, but you have months and even years to build relationships with these people. And while the focus of this chapter so far has been on outward appearances, a good working environment depends on real people bringing out the best in each other.

These tips will take you beyond the introductions and into the early months of your new job:

**Show interest.** Be open to and interested in all the people you meet at your new job. Really listen to them, whether they're instructing you on the fine art of not jamming the copy machine or telling you about their volleyball league. Ask questions, make eye contact, try to remember specific details. People appreciate and respond to those who are sincere, engaging, and curious. Conversely, the quickest way to turn others off is to appear self-centered and aloof.

**Be generous, but not too generous.** Give compliments, offer to buy a round of coffee, bring in treats for the staff room. But don't do any of these things too early or too much or you may come across as insincere or desperate. Acceptable for these early days: "Cute kid!" or "Nice spreadsheet!" Unacceptable: "You have great eyes!" or "You're the best boss ever!"

**Project a positive attitude.** Make sure that your net contribution to the office atmosphere is positive. Positive, energetic, professional, eager to work—all of these are traits of successful people. You might not always feel full of pep, but it's important to act like you're happy at your job and ready for business. In fact, you'll often find that acting energetic will improve your mood and actually give you the energy you need.

**Respect your coworkers' time and expertise**. You will probably need a lot of help figuring out office procedures and protocols. Asking for guidance from coworkers is one way to get to know them. Quick requests for recommendations—the best deli, the nearest dry cleaners, a good gym—can be great conversation starters. If you need something that will take more than a few minutes of a coworker's time, however, ask if you can set up an appointment. That way he or she will know that you value his or her expertise and time.

**Accept invitations.** In these early days on the job, you want to accept as many invitations as possible. It might be tempting to do a solo lunch so you can study your employee manual, but the most important thing to do at this stage is to connect with the people you work with. One cautionary note, however: If the conversation during these outings with colleagues heads towards gossip, be aware of your position as the new kid on the block and maintain neutrality. The trick is to be sociable without getting sucked into a clique.

**Connect with all players.** While support staff (receptionists, secretaries, administrative assistants, office managers, and IT support) might have smaller paychecks than CEOs, they are generally very powerful people in the company. Why? They have the keys (literally) to the supply closet, have access to top management, and can get you assistance when you need it fast. When you're on deadline and the copy machine goes down, you want the go-to person to be there for you. If you've cultivated a good relationship with him or her, you'll be in good shape. Also, support staff knows everything about everything: They can tell you which days the boss is in a good mood and can even help you minimize a mistake if you've made one.

Winning over coworkers isn't about faking them out, but about putting your best self forward. It will help you professionally and personally if you showcase your best attributes in these early days on the job. As American author Kurt Vonnegut once said, "We are what we pretend to be, so we must be careful about what we pretend to be." If you want to be poised, articulate, personable, engaged and engaging, organized, and positive, act like you already are that way. This attitude and way of being will serve you well beyond those early, first impressions and soon you'll see it's not just about how others see you, but about how you see yourself.

## CHAPTER 18

# UNDERSTANDING YOUR ORGANIZATION

The robots of this world can judge how good a work situation is with hard, quantitative data: Add salary (X) to benefits (Y) and advancement potential (Z), then divide by commute time (C). That's it. The job is good if it pays well, offers a fancy title, and doesn't take two hours and three trains to reach. But experienced professionals will tell you that the feel of the company is critical to job satisfaction. Yep, the feel. Or, in office speak, the company culture.

Each company has a unique personality, composed of its values, structures, and behaviors. When you first get the job and begin to develop the skills and procedures that relate to your position, you'll also start to figure out the organization's culture. More importantly, you'll begin to understand how you interact with this culture.

It's kind of like moving to a new country: Some of the traditions and expressions will seem familiar immediately, while others become clear with time and translation. Because job satisfaction directly relates to how well the organization's personality meshes with your own, you'll want to get the lay of the land early on.

Consider this chapter your guide to understanding your organization. We'll provide a thorough definition of organizational culture, map out how you can assess your organization's personality, and offer tips on how to work with it.

## Two ears, one mouth

There's an old saying that we have two ears and one mouth because we're meant to listen twice as much as we speak. Keep that saying in mind as you navigate the first weeks and months of your new job. Interviews are meant for showcasing your achievements, impressing everyone with your knowledge, and just plain selling yourself. But after the interview is over and you're the new kid on the block, it's time to show how well you adapt, which means more watching and listening and less talking.

Here's how to start out right:

**Watch.** Observe body language and how people in the company interact. Where do people gather? Who are the leaders? How much space do employees give each other? Is it a heads-down environment—everyone working quietly in their cubicles or offices—or more open and collaborative? Do people take breaks? What are the workday norms—is it a 9 to 5 office that really shuts down at 5:00 p.m. or do people tend to come early, work late, and take work home?

**Listen.** Listen to the way people communicate with each other. Do they share ideas freely? Is it an outspoken environment or more reserved? Casual or formal? How do colleagues talk about their work? How do they talk about customers, coworkers, and management?

**Ask questions.** Learning about the company and your new job can feel like you're drinking from a firehose, but try and absorb as much as possible without getting overwhelmed. Ask questions that will help you understand the company better as well as your role in it. Carry a pad of paper and pencil with you so you can take good notes of everything you learn. Remember that no one expects you to know everything right off the bat so they'll see your questions as a sign of interest and a willingness to learn and adapt. It's better to ask early, too, because at some point you will be expected to "just know." Another way to gather valuable information is by reading—read the employee manual, company literature, the website, and all emails that come through your inbox.

**Implement what you learn.** Once you get the lay of the land you'll be confident you know what's expected of you. Then it's simply a matter of doing it. Look to the leaders of the company as models of job performance. You'll find leaders— engaged, enthusiastic, and productive people—in every department and at every level, from management to support staff.

By observing the ways of others, you'll soon get a sense of how to operate successfully within the organization's environment.

## Company culture

As we mentioned in the introduction, company culture is a product of a combination of values, structures, and behaviors. You'll pick up on some aspects of your new workplace's culture as early as the first interview. The environment itself reveals a lot about the company's values: From the layout of the office to the casual interactions between colleagues you'll find clues to deciphering the unwritten "codes" of culture. Here are some ideas to help guide your assessment:

**Mission and vision.** Is there a clear, shared company mission? Do your coworkers speak positively about the company and its leadership? Does every employee feel invested in the future of the organization? Successful, dynamic businesses depend on a shared vision.

**Expectations and support.** Are standards and expectations clearly defined and attainable? Do supervisors encourage and nurture employees' success on the job by giving timely and constructive feedback on their work? Are mentors available? Is there a clear evaluation/annual review system? These qualities not only foster your ongoing professional success but also ensure that you're respected and that your contributions are valued.

**Physical office structure.** Does the office layout say hierarchy or anarchy (or, more likely, something in-between)? An open floor plan with shared workspaces hints at a collaborative, non-hierarchical organization, while rows of cubicles surrounded by closed-door offices suggest a highly stratified environment.

**Work habits and hours.** What are the standard hours employees keep? What are the productivity expectations? Do your coworkers have working lunches and "breaks"? Are employees expected to volunteer for additional projects? Get a sense of what everybody's doing early on so you can adjust your pace accordingly.

**Communication.** What are the most common modes of communication used within the office? Face to face? Email? Phone? Little sticky notes? What do you see in meetings? Does one person control the agenda? When there is tension, do the people involved treat each other respectfully? Less important are the number of disagreements around the office as the way they are resolved.

**State of the staff room.** Is the staff room a hub of interaction or basically unused? If the lunchroom is a gathering place, take advantage of the time to meet and get to know more people. Oftentimes these informal conversations are inspiring and will help you recharge. Of course, some staff rooms breed whining or, worse, gossiping. If this is the case, respectfully avoid it as much as you can.

**Flexibility.** Does the company allow or even encourage flexible work hours? Can employees job share or reduce their full time status if they want to? Remember, these options may not seem relevant to you now, but circumstances change. The more a company recognizes that you have a life outside of work, the better.

**Resources.** Resources might include technology, postage, food, and office supplies. How liberal is the company with its stuff? How does one go about procuring a toner cartridge? What kind of documentation is necessary? Whatever your company's "available resource" profile, be sensitive to norms regarding office supplies.

**Turnover.** Do people tend to stick around or does the organization have a more fluid workforce? Of the longstanding employees, who are leaders in the organization?

There may be other elements involved in your particular organization's personality, but these are the most common to consider. Once you have a clear reading you'll see how you can work within the culture.

## Working within your organization's culture

Your office's culture will have a profound effect on your life at work and outside of it. Expect that the organization is going to influence you at least as much as you influence it, if not more.

As with other parts of your life, some of the most important rules are the unspoken ones. Follow the ones that add to a positive environment. For example, your company may value the holiday party, and for that reason alone, you should, too. So, if you're trying to decide whether to attend the holiday party or not, think about the impression you'll make if you do attend (or the impression you'll leave behind if you don't show up.) It's tough to give up a Saturday evening in December, but it's worthwhile and will likely mean a lot to those you work with.

Some norms, of course, are better broken or ignored. Even the most positive workplaces might contain a group that thrives on gossip, undermining, or other detrimental behaviors. Of course you'll want to avoid spreading gossip or getting too close with anyone known for spreading gossip. If you detect a clique, be friendly with the members in a way that is respectful but keeps you a safe distance from becoming part of the group. That way you won't end up inadvertently alienating yourself from colleagues outside the clique. Other bad habits to avoid include complaining, bad-mouthing, and lax expense accounting on business trips. If the norms at your organization are too far afield of your best judgment, you might want to consider switching jobs.

While there are guidelines and tools to help you assess your organization's personality, there's no simple, objective formula to predict how soon you'll feel like "one of the natives." If you're lucky, you've landed in an organization that feels like a good match, a place where you can learn and grow comfortably. However, even an imperfect match can be instructive. When you learn to work well within a challenging culture, you hone skills that are incredibly helpful in the long run. Keep your overall personal and professional goals in mind. You'll be able to learn from all experiences and apply the knowledge you've gained to a long and rewarding career.

## CHAPTER 19

# REALISTIC EXPECTATIONS

You've heard of sticker shock and culture shock, but here's a new condition you should know about: Reality shock. Reality shock is the state many recent graduates find themselves in a week or so into their first job, when their expectations for the job collide head-on with the reality of the organization's expectations of them. So if your eyes ache from the flash of the copier machine and the blur of entering data, know this: Everyone starts somewhere.

Open up a copy of Forbes or Fortune and scan the pages. All those high-powered executives? You can bet that almost every one of them put in their time filing, copying, entering data, and doing all the tasks considered, well, boring. The vast majority of professionals paid their dues in the early years of their career.

However, articles and stories that celebrate successful people often gloss over the boring stuff and head straight for the critical plays, breakthroughs, and stellar accomplishments. We want to hear about someone collating and three-hole punching about as much as we want to hear Uncle Dave's "when I was a kid I walked three miles each way to school stories." And when most of what we know about the working world is based on television or magazine profiles or even textbooks, it's not surprising that most of us suffer from at least a little reality shock.

We hope this chapter will help you set realistic expectations for yourself, understand the most common causes of reality shock, and see what you're doing now as one step in a successful career.

## The importance of having realistic expectations

Did you ever get so excited for a gathering or a big trip that when the actual event came it was anticlimactic? Not that it was bad, but it just wasn't what you imagined somehow. That gap between anticipated excitement and reality can be a bummer. And even if you are generally an optimistic and motivated person, it's not uncommon to get so excited by the job search and hiring process that when you start the daily work it seems, well, just like work. Contributing to this feeling is the great sense of accomplishment you get when you graduate: Here I am world! Qualified! Degreed! Skilled! Energetic! Master of my field! And then someone asks you to change the toner.

If you feel this reality shock you are by no means alone. In fact, the most common complaint of new hires after two weeks on the job is that it isn't what they expected. The good news is it's no longer a complaint after two months on the job. The message here is clear: Give it time. In the meantime, learn about the most frequent causes of new job dissatisfaction.

## Employer needs/new employee needs

It's natural to come out of school ready to "hit the ground running" and prove yourself. You are smart and motivated and eager to become an integral part of the team. Your employer probably hired you for all of these reasons and will ultimately be happy to let you work to your fullest potential. However, it's possible that your needs and your employer's needs in these early days are not the same. It's not necessarily that they are at odds with each other, but more that they're operating at different speeds. You want to run with your talents and take an active role in the organization; your supervisor needs to train you and evaluate your skills and level of commitment. The organization is investing time, energy, and money in you and needs to see evidence that you're invested, too.

You can expect, then, that the early days will involve training and sometimes repetitive tasks. Employers generally like to ease new employees into the scene and provide them with background information as well as a chance to get used to the office norms. Some organizations' training programs are very comprehensive, designed to teach every aspect of the organization to every employee.

Whatever the reason for your new-hire job duties, remember they hired you because they're really busy and need help. Right now you might be stapling and changing the occasional ink cartridge, but once they see you care about the job you'll be on your way to doing other things that are more in line with your goals. Here are some things to keep in mind on these early days on the job:

**Everyone starts somewhere.** Even the CEO has spent time copying, collating, and entering data.

**Demonstrate initiative.** Volunteer for projects and tasks. Your main goal at this point, after all, is to get to know the ins and outs of your new organization.

**Be positive.** Your positive outlook and willingness to contribute will be noticed.

**Do a good job.** This one might be intuitive, but it bears repeating. Whatever your assigned task, do it carefully and do it well. Every action should convey your attention to details and ability to produce quality work.

**Be patient with yourself.** It can be frustrating to learn the ropes at a new job. It's typical to make mistakes in these early days. On top of that, you may feel slow and inefficient. Don't worry. You will get the hang of it. Focus on one task at a time.

If you need to ask about the tasks you've been assigned, try to begin the question with an "I understand" statement. For example, say "I understand the value of this training process, but I'm curious about when I can expect to transition to other tasks." This will show your supervisor that you're ready to move on without making it seem like you're resistant to instruction.

So far we've assumed you might be dealing with the reality shock that comes from not being given what you think is meaningful, challenging work. There are other types of shock, though. Sometimes you'll land in an organization that is so slammed with work that you get all sorts of interesting, high-stakes projects—and no training. A situation like this can make even the most competent person feel completely overwhelmed.

To make the most of it, ask questions of available coworkers, and try to learn by example. It's a challenge to face such a steep learning curve, but it can be incredibly rewarding in the end. In this case, your employer's need—to get someone who will learn and produce fast—might be a great jump start to your career with the organization. And chances are, you'll end up feeling like an integral player in the organization's success.

| New Employee Needs | Organization Needs (supervisor and coworkers) |
|---|---|
| Challenging Tasks | To know that the new employee is competent |
| Autonomy | Evidence that new employee is trustworthy and understands his/her function in the organization |
| To feel valued | Proven commitment and loyalty |
| To feel he/she belongs and is liked | Evidence new employee is making an effort to fit in and respects others' time and space |

## Other common causes of reality shock

In addition to the gap between the employer's needs and your own, there may be some other unexpected realities of work. Following are some of the most common surprises:

**Bosses.** Bosses are more demanding than college professors, and in the workplace success is often judged simply on results. This is in contrast to college, where success is often evaluated according to product and process. In other words, a professor might care if you've invested a lot of time and energy in a paper or project, but a boss is just going to look at the final product.

**Salary.** Many graduates overestimate their initial salary potential as well as the frequency and rate of promotions.

**Good Tip:** GOOD TO KNOW

*"Know how long your position has been around and how many people have held it."*

~ Mary K., California

Your position in the organization might be newly created or it could have a history. If it's a new position, you'll want to know so you can help define expectations. If it's been around, you'll want to know about your predecessor's successes and failures so you can learn from them.

Raises, too, are on average much lower than television or corporate lore would have us believe. Your workplace's human resources department is a good place to start asking what standard promotion and salary practices are for that organization. You can also look online for regional norms if you want to get an outside perspective.

**Workspace.** Another sometimes jarring reality is the workspace you'll have when you first start. A cubicle, a corner of the staff room, a shared table. If you're disappointed with your placement, just keep in mind that your status is a function of how you see yourself, not where you sit or what computer you've been assigned.

**Work hours.** Other common surprises include time demands. You might be hired for what seems like a forty-hour a week job, but end up putting in many more hours learning the ropes and doing what it takes to complete the tasks you've been given. You will get more efficient as time goes on, but it's also possible that the organization survives on lots of people working lots of hours. Or even just a few people working lots and lots of hours. If that's the case, you'll either get acclimated to the time spent on the job or decide to shift gears.

**Fitting in.** If one of the other feelings you experience is a lack of a sense of belonging, rest assured that this is typical at first. Your new coworkers are busy and won't necessarily go out of their way to meet the new person. But take heart. With time you'll get to know each other and the relationships will develop naturally. Do what you can to connect with them: Ask them questions about their interests, invite them to join you for lunch, and accept invitations they extend to you.

Whatever your experiences in the first weeks and months of your new job, try to keep your ultimate goals in mind. At some point in the not-so-distant future, you'll be doing the work you want to be doing.

# GO BEYOND AVERAGE

## CHAPTER 20

Average. Even the word is boring. Kind of nasally and slow, like a whine. It's no surprise, then, that no one wants to be average. We want below average cholesterol and above average intelligence, but even that seems a little dull. Who wants to go to a restaurant or a doctor with just an "above average" reputation? Who wants to be labeled "above average"? Bleh. It's as good as saying "not excellent."

So let's get rid of that word right here. In your work life you want to be way beyond average. Not even in the same realm. Instead, you'll be excellent. Superior. Remarkable. You want to advance your knowledge and experience (and, yes, your salary) so you need to go beyond the basic job description on a regular basis. A dynamic, fulfilling career is comprised of many daily decisions to exceed expectations.

Starting your job with the mission of proving to both your supervisors and yourself that you've got the right stuff will instill a habit of excellence. You'll become so accustomed to welcoming challenges and doing your best that remarkable job performance will be your norm. And you'll find that the energy you give will come back to you.

Now, the advice in this chapter is common sense, the stuff of Abe Lincoln stories and more than one commencement address. But there's a reason these tips are repeated in various forms by successful people: Going beyond expectations is what separates the "average" and "above average" professional from the "very successful" one.

## Work a full day

We know, we know. This one seems painfully obvious. However, even though conventional wisdom says to work a full day at your job if you want to excel, managers still report that many employees arrive a little late and leave a little early. And take a lot of breaks. Now, circadian rhythm and psychological studies may show that flexible hours plus a nap in the middle of the day boosts productivity and efficiency, but let's just say that most of the working world hasn't caught up to this way of thinking.

People notice if you arrive late and leave early, and they really, really notice if you show up for a meeting with sleep creases on your face. No matter how much you're actually getting done, timeliness can't be underestimated. If you get to the office early and leave a little late, you'll establish yourself as someone who is committed and hardworking. And that's the kind of getting noticed you want.

## Do your job well

Whatever you're doing, take pride in your work. Two sayings come to mind here: "All work is meaningful" and "Way leads onto way." And while these might sound pat when you're doing double data entry and extreme filing, they're cliché because they're true. We all start somewhere, and if it's in document shredding, well, be a fast, thorough (and ethical!) shredder. Write a book about it—*Zen and the Art of Document Shredding*—or a comedy routine. Or come up with a better method of shredding and patent it. Or simply finish the shredding early and volunteer to take on a task that will really challenge you and showcase your talents.

## Take the initiative

One great way to demonstrate your willingness to work hard as well as your yet-to-be-fully-revealed capabilities is to take the initiative and volunteer for projects, committees, and additional training. These volunteer efforts could mean taking on gigantic projects—rewriting a computer program, for instance, or creating a style manual—or even offering assistance with the little tasks that aren't glamorous but simply need to get done, like binding a report or running copies.

**Treat Every Project Like a Raise Depends on It** To Do!

Every day, and with every task, ask yourself if you're working to your full potential. Sure, you're past tryouts (the interviews and probationary period) and have "made the team," but you still need to prove your worth to the organization on a daily basis. This will benefit you and the organization you work for. People who treat every task and project like a raise depends on it tend to have a higher rate of job satisfaction and fulfillment. And, on top of it all, they are more likely to earn rewards like promotions and raises.

Taking on tasks outside your job "requirements," whether those tasks are challenging or remedial, will help you learn more about the organization, develop your skills, and establish strong relationships with your supervisors and colleagues.

## Make the most of your mistakes

Superior job performance includes dealing with mistakes in a constructive way. The below average employee covers up or blows off mistakes; the average employee minimizes his or her mistakes by passing or maybe "sharing" the buck; the excellent employee takes responsibility for his or her mistakes, learns from them, and moves on. It's not a question if you'll make mistakes but how you'll deal with them when you do. If you're up front about an error, reflect on it, and self-correct, the mistake itself won't be nearly as memorable as the lasting impression of your integrity and dedication to doing your job right.

## Contribute positively to the company

All employees contribute to the company, but not all add to it. Get in the habit of asking yourself if you are adding positively to the environment. Before making a statement or asking a question in a meeting, for instance, ask yourself, "Is this going to add and help or will it distract from the purpose? Am I offering solutions or problems?" When talking with others in the staff room, ask yourself, "Am I adding something positive here?"

The basic questions to ask yourself are, *What are my intentions?* and *What are the possible implications of this statement/action?* Checking in with yourself on a regular basis will help you maintain a consistently positive role in your company. We're not saying, however, that you need to be a yes man or yes woman. On the contrary, successful people often need to question the status quo or their colleagues' and supervisor's ideas. But if your intentions and methods are good, you'll know how to add in a productive, meaningful way.

## Take care of yourself...

...or you're no help to anyone else. Being a successful professional takes a lot of energy. In order to do your work well you need to take care of yourself, too. So while we recommend volunteering for projects and committees, and certainly advise you to expect to dedicate many hours on and off the job working, it's also very important to take care of your personal needs. Sleep, for instance, is not an optional activity. Being your best at work means being your best, period. Alert. Focused. Personable. Even fun. So if you do choose to sign up for an additional project, do it well. Don't overextend yourself—you want to come across as professional, competent, and motivated rather than frazzled.

If you're lucky you're surrounded by supervisors and colleagues who share a desire to be way beyond average. In your company, the norm might be excellence and so "meeting the standard" means working at a very high level all the time. Such work environments can be incredibly supportive of both the individual's and the company's needs, inspiring every employee to work beyond his or her potential. Whatever your actual job circumstances, set high expectations for your own performance and you'll always be better off for having done so.

# YOU, ONLINE

## CHAPTER 21

You've heard the idea that everyone is connected to everyone else by just six degrees of separation? Well, make that just two degrees of separation, thanks to social media such as Facebook, LinkedIn, and Twitter. Because of this, your online presence—and the relationships you build through social networking—is vital to building your career.

The majority of people still find jobs and get hired through personal connections. Social media is your route to making more personal connections—and to making them more, well, personal. The old saw "it's not what you know, it's who you know" has morphed into "it's not just who you know, it's who knows you." Which leads us to a critical question: What do people know about you? If they know you're skilled, trustworthy, and hardworking, they will be happy to help you connect with others. Having a strong network not only gets you the job—it also gives you the opportunity to exchange ideas and knowledge with other professionals.

Now is the time to create a professional online presence and start building valuable connections. In this chapter we'll discuss the major social media sites and how you can use them to grow professionally.

## Social media
Grandpa, what's Facebook? For as long as there's been social media, there have been people predicting its death. As of the printing of this book, however, it's still very much around. In fact, Facebook, as of this moment, has 1.1 billion active users. LinkedIn, a professional networking site, has over 260 million users. On LinkedIn, users post their profiles, including job experience and education, resumes, and interests. LinkedIn individual members use the site to make professional connections and exchange ideas. Companies use LinkedIn to find new hires. If Facebook is casual Friday—or very, very casual Saturday night—LinkedIn is business-attire Monday. Facebook lends itself to informal, personal exchanges; LinkedIn is your best reflection of your professional self. Another popular means of staying connected is Twitter, which people use to post short updates or to track their friends, favorite celebrities, and organizations. There are countless other social media outlets to explore.

## Establishing and maintaining an online presence
You've probably been using Facebook, Twitter, and Instagram for years and have already built an online presence. In this section we'll discuss how to manage that online presence so that it *helps* your professional life.

**First, take stock of your current online profile.** Here's a handy exercise: Google yourself to see what others can easily find out about you. Odds are, you've already done this exercise on someone else. See anything interesting? If you end up with

## Who are you online?

Your online personality may be a factor in whether or not you're hired, fired, or promoted. Consider these two examples: One applicant for a marketing assistant job had all the qualifications, but made a bad first impression before she even set foot in the interview room. Her interviewer Googled her and discovered, among other things, a blog post filled with profanity. She did not get the job. Unfair? Possibly. But it's certainly not an isolated case. Another example is a chef who ranted about his employer on his blog, and made sarcastic comments online that damaged the restaurant's reputation. He was fired immediately. Everything you post online—and even those things posted about you—can potentially help or sabotage your career.

a few innocuous results (your little league batting average or a graduation picture, for instance), you are in a great position, as you can simply monitor your online presence and make sure nothing gets linked to your name that you don't want. You'll also want to build on that presence, which we'll get to in a moment.

**Next, delete and bury if necessary.** If you do have blog posts, pictures, or other items online that could potentially embarrass you or limit your chances of finding and keeping a job in the future, delete them, if possible. It's not likely that you can remove the images or content from every source, but you can try to bury it by increasing favorable content. For instance, some people use LinkedIn, Twitter, or Pinterest because activity on those websites makes their most relevant and recent content most visible. It's no different than what many companies do to help their brand. You can do the same thing. Another way to bury negative items is to create a new website or blog and add to it regularly.

**Finally, take control of your professional online identity.** What do you want connections, colleagues, employers and potential employers to learn about you when they search for you online? (Yes, they check.) Here's how to build a professional online presence:

1. **A good first career move is to join the organizations relevant to your profession—or the profession you'd like to have.** Sign up for relevant Facebook groups, Listservs, or other email groups and check them regularly. Make sure you consider all groups that might benefit you professionally: National, regional, and local professional organizations; alumni groups; and specialty interests that relate to your current or future professional goals.

2. **Create a profile on a professional networking site, such as LinkedIn.** Upload your resume and request recommendations from professors or previous employers. Approach online requests for favors such as recommendations just as you would in the real world: Show that you value the person's time and assistance, be specific about your request, and follow up with a thank you email or note.

3. **Make Facebook a positive or neutral force in your professional life.**
   Decide who you want to view your Facebook profile. Clean up your
   profile, posts, and page if possible. Check your privacy settings. Facebook
   is notorious for changing privacy settings regularly and not providing
   very clear directions about dealing with those changes. Luckily, if you
   Google "Facebook" and "privacy settings" you'll find plenty of tips on how
   to tighten your privacy settings. Privacy online, however, is always best
   considered an oxymoron.

## Making connections

Both Facebook and LinkedIn are excellent for
networking and provide a window that up to a
few years ago wasn't available. Remember that
the rules of engaging professionally online are
the same as they are in the real world: Introduce
yourself and demonstrate your respect for the
person's time by keeping your messages short
and by not flooding the person with requests
or information. Be gracious, too. For example,
some people limit their LinkedIn connections to
a small circle of very well known, highly trusted
individuals, and will not accept your invitation
to link up until they get to know you better.
Also, consider your situation carefully before
friending a boss or colleague on Facebook.
Do you want that extra level of connection
with them? What are potential drawbacks and
benefits of being Facebook friends with people at your particular workplace?

> **Make an Impression with Online Posts or Tweets**
>
> **Consider This ...**
>
> **Job recruiters are impressed by:**
> - Affiliations with professional organizations
> - Volunteerism
>
> **Job recruiters are turned off by:**
> - References to drugs, alcohol, and sex
> - Rude or disparaging remarks about others
> - Poor grammar and spelling mistakes
> - Self-centered posts
>
> *Source: Jobvite, 2012*

Ultimately, networking—making connections, linking, friending—is all about
relationships. And the best relationships are mutually enriching. Consider your
role in your network: there will be times when you'll need to call on others for
assistance, advice, and favors and other times when you'll be the one assisting,
advising, and doing what you can to help somebody else out.

## Finding a job

Social media can be an essential means not just to finding a job, but to finding
the right job. From a simple Facebook status update or tweet: "Anyone know of
any accounting positions open in Austin?" to a more targeted LinkedIn search
for a position in a particular department in the organization of your dreams, you
have a powerful job search tool literally at your fingertips.

If you find yourself needing a job, first get the word out. Post what you're looking
for and follow up any tips you get from people with an update or thank you. If
you find yourself wanting another job—but are not ready to tell your colleagues
or supervisor that you want to move on—you might have to be more targeted
about getting the word out. You don't want your boss to find out and have, at
best, an awkward conversation and, at worst, a "burned bridge."

Next, search for companies and organizations that interest you and determine if you have any personal connections to someone working there. For example, you might see that one of your contacts on LinkedIn is connected with someone who works in the field you want to get into. You might contact that person—a so-called "second-degree contact," akin to a "friend of a friend"— and request information or let him or her know of your interest. Note: Common practice is to limit such messages to second-degree contacts. In other words, reach out to a contact of a contact, but not a contact's contact's contact. Even if you don't have connections to an organization, you can get a lot of information about it and potential job openings by searching its website and following it on Twitter and Facebook.

Remember to update and thank people who help you out in the process of finding a job. They'll appreciate the follow up.

## Social networking and the workplace

You might have a job that requires you to be plugged into Facebook and Twitter all day, but if it's not part of the job description you should probably avoid social media activity while you're on the clock. We know one person who was fired after he called in sick the same day he posted on Facebook pictures of himself soaking up the sun at the beach. Another acquaintance was such an active Facebook status updater that it was hard to imagine she was able to get any work done in between the updates. (A colleague, tired of having his email requests to her ignored, once sent a Facebook notice from his cubicle next door: "When you're done with Facebook, would you mind going over the edits?")

Social networking is very much alive. It's a powerful force in the social and professional lives of countless millions of people. It can backfire—being tagged in those pictures from Cabo, for instance—but follow common sense and social networking can be an incredible enriching and positive force in your professional life.

## CHAPTER 22

# WHAT YOUR COLLEGE HAS TO OFFER YOU NOW

Remember those long nights of studying and the way your eyes glazed over the pages of a text book at 2:00 a.m.? Remember how your hands cramped as you scribbled and scrawled over every possible surface of the test booklet during an exam? Well, for most graduates, those trials are over.

The tests and papers are filed away and you have one simple task remaining: Right click, add bookmark. No aches and pains. Just a simple keystroke or two and you enter into a world of opportunity, a world where experts offer you free or next-to-free financial advice, a world where everyone wants to help you find the job of your dreams and can actually help make that happen, a world of drastic discounts on auto insurance and even pizza. That's right...you have just bookmarked your alumni association's webpage.

Many people don't realize or take advantage of one of college's most important resources: its deep pool of graduates. If you're not connecting with them yet you're in for a very pleasant surprise when you find out how much you actually got for all the work you did in college: First, a degree and, now, access to all sorts of cool services as well as a dynamic network of alumni.

If the classroom represents *What* you know, your alumni association represents *who* you know. Any successful person will tell you that an education can open a lot of doors for you, but connections can open even more. One of the primary functions of the alumni association, after all, is to create and support a social and professional community based on a common background. It's difficult to overstate the benefits of taking part in such a community. In this chapter we'll tell you about the networking opportunities and other services alumni organizations provide and how you can tap into them.

## Networking
The primary purpose of alumni groups is to nurture graduates' ties to their alma mater. And while the buildings, quads, and fountains of the college campus continue to inspire a sense of belonging in the graduate, it's the people who make a school's environment truly rich and lasting. Alumni organizations extend the experience by offering graduates frequent and varied opportunities to connect with other alumni. Some people are motivated by the social aspects of such a group, others motivated by the career-boosting advantages. Most seek a combination of both. Here are some of the networking possibilities available:

**Alumni clubs/chapters.** Alumni associations usually have smaller regional clubs/chapters so graduates can get to know other alumni who live nearby. The only prerequisites for belonging, besides being an alum, are signing up and, in some cases, paying dues. The more active of these groups might organize charity events, college recruitment efforts, lectures and seminars, book groups, opera outings, holiday parties, tailgate parties, and other sports-centered events. Some of the less active clubs might be content to host an occasional alumni happy hour at the local restaurant. It's a good idea to check out at least a few of the events—you might see some old friends from school and you could end up meeting some new ones. Also, these casual get-togethers are a great way to network on a regular basis.

## Benefits of Networking

What, exactly, are the benefits of networking? Why go to a meet-and-greet when you could be hanging out at home watching your favorite TV show? If you tap into an effective and supportive network, you'll...

**Discover** valuable resources, new methods and practice in your field, and unique approaches to problems.

**Exchange ideas** with people in and outside of your practice in order to enlarge your understanding.

**Get advice** from experienced professionals.

**Get inspired** by meeting energetic, creative people (after all, none of you is staying home watching TV).

**Increase your visibility** if you're building up a business or clientele.

**Get leads** on new clients, job opportunities, employees, etc.

**Shared interest groups.** Do you want to work for a service organization in a developing country? Are you starting a technology business? Do you ski? Your alumni website can point you to all sorts of ways you can connect with like-minded people. You might find an online discussion group centered on your area of study or, in some cases, an alumni chapter in your town that's made up of people who majored in the same field. These groups can provide valuable support as you take on new challenges. They can also, of course, introduce you to others who might know someone who knows someone who's looking to invest in a promising new company. Or someone who knows of a perfect job opportunity for you. Or—even better—someone who knows how you can score tickets to a sold-out show.

**Mentor programs.** Some associations match experienced and novice professionals. The volunteer mentor gets the satisfaction of helping an up-and-coming young person establish him or herself. The up-and-coming young person (that's you) gets the benefit of years of wisdom and experience at the beginning of his or her career. (Also, said newly graduated professional might meet a mentor who's looking for a bright, capable person to hire.)

**Singles groups.** Another important aspect of life after graduation for many people is meeting interesting singles. Some associations now offer singles activities—whitewater rafting, anyone?—as well as password-protected message boards and similar sites.

Whatever your field of interest or motivation for getting involved with your association, networking invariably broadens one's horizons and prospects. Another way to tap into the your alumni association is through the services it offers.

## Services

Many of the services available serve the dual purpose of networking, but we include them separately because networking is not their primary function. The following is a list of services your alumni organization might offer:

**Career planning services.** From password-protected job boards to access to informational interviews with alumni, the career planning services available through some schools' associations are phenomenal. There are workshops, individual career counseling, and even resume tutorials and critiques. Some colleges charge for these services, but the fees are minimal and a great investment for the cost.

**Relocation support.** If you're relocating it's a good idea to check with the alumni chapter in your new region. You might find people eager to guide you through the ins and outs of your new location, whether that means introducing you to a great real estate agent or giving you tips on the local scene. Some national alumni associations even have programs to assist spouses and children with their relocation issues.

**Business development.** You can post information about your business, recruit employees, and even get a grant or loan, depending on your alumni association. People starting new companies, by the way, can get a lot of free advice and press by simply contacting other alumni.

**Travel.** Want to attend a Civil War lecture at the site of a significant battle? Feel like going to Italy for a few weeks this spring? Again, you might be surprised at how many cool travel opportunities your association offers. As a large organization, it has the clout to recruit expert guides and lecturers as well as the buying power to qualify for discounted travel expenses. (That doesn't mean that all alumni travel is en masse.) And if for some reason your college doesn't offer the cool seminars and group tours, your membership in the local chapter can probably garner you a personal discount on airfare or travel-related expenses.

**Continuing education.** For those of you who never wanted to leave college, take heart! You can keep learning and this time you don't need to suffer the writer's

### Networking Etiquette TIP

Here are some rules for networking with class:

**Remember: Person First.** Approach people as interesting individuals, not job titles. The person you introduce yourself to at the meet-and-greet might end up being a great client, but only if they feel respected and liked.

**Conversation Sells More Than Selling.** In other words, engage with people authentically and know when to talk shop and when to talk about other things.

**Respect Others' Time.** Everyone is busy. Be graciously aware of the other person's time constraints. Also, send a thank you card when someone does you the favor of giving up their time to help you.

block and hand cramps of finals week. If you live close to campus you may be eligible to audit classes. Or you might find that your local chapter recruits great lecturers for their meetings. Some schools post free online lectures for alumni. Others host research databases. There are countless ways you can continue your education and the first place to look for opportunities is the association webpage.

**Discounts.** Oh, yes. The discounts alone might be worth those tuition checks. Here's just a sampling of discounts we found while perusing a variety of alumni associations: pizza, luxury cars, life insurance, eye exams, carpet cleaning, airfare, credit card interest rates, auto insurance, pet food, college credits. Basically, if it's something you pay for you might find you can pay less for it by flashing your alum ID card.

Whew. That's a lot of goods for a simple action. Right click, bookmark, and all of a sudden you're basking in the sun in the mountains of Italy, networking by email with a big time venture capitalist, discussing everything from investments to the current basketball season. OK, so maybe we overstate the benefits of this resource, the alumni association. On the other hand, where else will you find an organization that offers access to prime career development services as well as frequent networking opportunities (and, of course, great tailgate parties)?

# WHAT YOU HAVE TO OFFER YOUR COLLEGE

## CHAPTER 23

One of the great pleasures in life is watching the new wing on the student union building take shape with your name etched in the stone cornice above the entryway. You know that generations of students will benefit from your generosity. Other satisfying ways to contribute to your alma mater are establishing a professorship or donating an electron microscope.

That time will come. For the present, you're probably more concerned with monthly expenses than architectural drawings of your legacy. However, every philanthropist starts somewhere; what matters is not the size of the contribution or the form it takes, but the very act of contributing.

Recent graduates may be shocked by how soon solicitations show up from their college alumni association. The cap and gown are barely put away when the first brochure appears in the mailbox. Or the friendly voice sounds on the telephone: "Hello, Ms. So-and-so? This is Sophie from Your University." After you realize the student representative is really calling for you and not your mother, the shock kicks in: This is my new world. Adult. Alum. Pledge drives.

But then you realize it's not about giving in to or dodging from work-study students. It's about staying connected with your college and shaping its future. You know how you benefit from maintaining contact (see Chapter 15); here are some ways you can give back to the college community, and only a couple of them relate to money.

## Maintaining contact

We outlined some of the perks of staying in touch with your college and alumni association in the previous chapter. Your college benefits from this continued relationship, too. First, even your basic personal information and updates can add to the larger statistical picture that informs program direction and funding: Who graduates from which department, what they do post-graduation, how they apply their degree to their lives outside of school, etc. Also, and more importantly, your continued involvement builds on the network that supports current and former students as well as school departments and programs. You rely on the network and the network relies on you.

What's the best way to stay in contact? Well, the simplest way is by filling out and sending back the occasional forms that ask for your most recent information. Another easy way is to join the local alumni club/chapter and commit to attending a few events a year. If you want to be more involved, consider volunteering for your college or alumni association.

## Mentoring

Mentoring is a powerful way to stay connected to your college: You get the pleasure of sharing your skills and expertise, and the beneficiaries of your efforts get the assistance they need and will someday pass it on to others. Mentor programs vary in structure and size from college to college, but they all focus on connecting experienced professionals with up-and-coming professionals. Once you feel established in your career, think about the guidance you had (or would like to have had) as a student. Then, volunteer in a capacity that fits your knowledge and, of course, schedule. You might meet one-on-one with a student to discuss new research and opportunities in your shared field of study or you could assist students by providing informational interviews. Another helpful service you might offer is critiquing resumes and cover letters. If you're interested in career coaching, some alumni associations offer mentors training in how to help guide students in that area.

### Alumni Mentors...

GOOD TO KNOW

- Share their knowledge and expertise
- Offer guidance with internship opportunities and job searches
- Provide informational interviews
- Help connect students with professional organizations
- Give students on-the-job experience
- Coach students on interview and presentation skills
- Speak to large or small groups at high schools or other organizations about the college

Mentoring is a rewarding and flexible method of contributing to your college community. If you have an hour a week you can take part in an on-line Q and A or offer advice on a career search message board. If you have more time you can take on a larger role in the alumni network. The results of your energies won't be written in stone on the new student union building, but they will be just as long-lasting.

## Volunteer work

Are you itching to do something meaningful outside of your job? There comes a point in most people's careers when they're satisfied with the work they're doing but just need to add a little more to the greater community. If you fit this profile, consider contributing time to your college. As with mentoring, the extent of your involvement is up to you: Have an afternoon? Help out with the annual fund drive. Have a day? Help out at the new student orientation. Have grant-writing experience? Well, there's no end to the ways your school could put that to work.

Geography is not an issue, either. Even if you live far from your alma mater you can help out with recruitment or other efforts not tied to campus. Consider serving on the alumni association board of directors, for instance, or serving in a leadership position for your regional council/chapter.

## Financial support

So far we've gone over some of the ways you can support your college family. Now let's talk about how you can give financial support even as you're starting your career. We'll call it "philanthropy on a budget."

First, look to the easy ways to make frequent, smaller gifts to your alma mater. Some schools are affiliated with phone plans and credit cards that give a percentage of each expense to the institution. These plans might work for you, though it's important to do the math and see if you could save more by using another credit card but maybe put part of those saved dollars toward an annual gift to your alumni association. Other minor expenses include things like paying annual alumni dues (not all schools have dues) and purchasing school-related license plates.

### Why contribute?
*Consider This ...*

- You want up-and-coming students to have the same opportunities you had.

- Your gift has exponential potential. A strong base support builds on itself—colleges that can demonstrate they are already well-supported are more likely to secure even bigger contributions and grants.

- As your college and its reputation grows, so does the value of your degree.

If you have more to give, whether it's $10 or $100 or $1,000 or more, you have a few options for how to give. These include:

**Designated gifts:** You direct your gift to the department or program of your choosing.

**Unrestricted gifts:** You let the school—administration, department heads, or alumni association—decide the best use of your gift.

**Matching gifts:** Before you contribute, ask your human resources department if your company matches gifts. This is a great way to leverage your contributions.

### Where does the money go?
*Good To Know*

- Teaching and learning programs
- Student research support
- Scholarships and grants
- Recruitment efforts
- Orientation programs
- Chairs and professorships
- Facility and technology upgrades

Whatever you do, remember to keep your receipts so you can take advantage of all eligible tax deductions.

You'll find that there are many perks associated with giving back to your college family. From free sporting event tickets to access to college-owned housing around the world, your alumni association has come up with clever ways to keep you engaged and involved with your alma mater. And, you may even get tax deductions or more visibility, which can be very helpful if, say, you're an independent agent. When you stay connected you win and the college community—present and future—wins.